Surgery on the Shoulders of Giants

Letters from a doctor abroad

Saqib Noor

Kings X Press
78 Cromer Street
London
WC1H 8DR

www.kingsxpress.com

To my family – thank you for your unwavering support. Without you, I would still be lost.

To my surgical mentors - thank you for your wisdom and guidance over so many years. I will always use your highest standards as a benchmark for my future work.

To those who have encouraged me to write - thank you for your belief in me. You have inspired me to express myself outwardly, one letter at a time. I hope this book does justice to the faith you have placed in me.

To my patients - thank you for sharing your stories, struggles and successes with me, wherever I have travelled. I will always strive to improve as a doctor and serve you the best I can.

To those reading these letters - thank you for joining me on this lifelong journey.

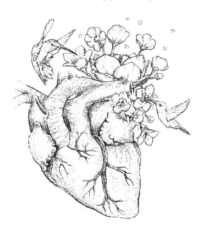

www.saqibnoor.com

Contents

CAMBODIA (2013)

ETHIOPIA (2016)

MYANMAR (2016)

HAITI (2017)

SELECTED PHOTOGRAPHS (2008-2017)

Preface

Dearest Readers,

This book is a simple collection of sporadic letters, written during my medical travels as a junior doctor, whilst I completed my training as an orthopaedic surgeon in the UK. The letters span ten years and describe visits to six countries in various capacities, ranging from emergency medical relief during the Haiti earthquake and Pakistan floods of 2010 to longer visits in South Africa and Cambodia, focussed on my surgical training and personal growth. More recently, my travels have involved contributing to surgical education programmes and international capacity building projects with brief visits to Ethiopia, Myanmar and a return to Haiti.

The letters were initially written to family and friends, happily describing my adventures and experiences, but they soon evolved into a deeply personal collection of inner thoughts, reflecting on all that I was learning, documenting vivid memories and life changing moments. Writing these letters has enabled me to truly evolve as a person and as a doctor whilst navigating the numerous challenges that we all ultimately face as we grow.

These letters were never written to be published in such a book format, nor indeed intended to be ever formally published at all. However, as I now complete my surgical training this year and hope to embark on further travels within this field, amalgamating this collection of writings feels simultaneously liberating and uncomfortably awkward. The letters remain a source of inspiration to me during my quieter or darker times, when I need motivation or focus. I publish them in the hope they can provide a similar solace or guidance to anyone else who reads them.

At the end of the book, I have included some selected photographs relating to the letters. I have excluded all photography of patients for their privacy and deepest respect. On the very rare occasion a patient's name is used in these letters, the name has been changed. No patient identifiable data is used within this book.

My heartfelt gratitude goes to all the people who have made my journeys so memorable over so many years. As always, I thank you, the reader, for also joining me on this journey.

With love always,

Saqib Noor

South Africa (2008-2009)

In 2008, I was giving serious thought to abandoning a career in surgery or indeed quitting medicine altogether. I qualified from medical school in 2004 and had completed basic surgical training, achieving the MRCS qualification (Membership of the Royal College of Surgeons). However, the uncertainty of obtaining higher surgical training in the UK, as well as a much deeper inner dialogue regarding my own ability to cope with the demands of being a surgeon, I decided to explore opportunities to work abroad as a stepping stone to either leaving medicine or battling on. I had always desired to experience healthcare in another part of the world and it genuinely felt the most natural time to fulfil this ambition.

With the assistance of a recruitment agency now known as Africa Health Placements, and months of endless paperwork, in August 2008, I eventually embarked on a year-long journey to Empangeni, Kwazulunatal, on the east coast of South Africa. My role was to be a trauma and orthopaedic officer, working in a busy tertiary hospital, receiving trauma cases from large areas of the state.

Although I had made enquiries with previous British doctors who had worked at the same hospital in a similar capacity, and researched as much as I could, I still remember having to frantically leave valuables behind at Heathrow airport as my luggage was wildly overweight, having a sense of both daunting nervousness and magical freedom as the airplane ascended from London into a most picturesque pink sky. I was younger then and truly had no idea what I would find or what the future held. It was only after a few months did I begin writing my letters home.

09.11.2008 – Sabono From The Work-Life Paradox!

Dearest Everyone,

Hello, Salaams and Greetings! Sabono! Unjani? (Hello, how are you? in Zulu!) Hoe gaandit? (Afrikaans) Embarrassingly, these are all the foreign phrases I have learnt so far! I am writing two months after arriving in South Africa and have found a moment to reflect on my experiences. Life is simultaneously hectic and tranquil here, and it is only now I feel I am truly settling in, adjusting to this new work-life paradox.

Work is gruelling in a generally understaffed orthopaedic department, especially compared to the volume of cases coming through and the overall staffing levels I am familiar with in England. My shifts begin sleepily at seven-thirty in the morning and end at five-thirty in the evening on most days. Every fifth day, I am on duty for thirty hours continuously, tremendously busy well into the evening and I am often awake throughout the night, reviewing injuries in the emergency room or operating on urgent cases. I manage to steal sleep under a flimsy blanket in the shared duty rooms with other doctors, or if those rooms are already occupied by fellow doctors competing for the beds, I curl up on the carpeted floor of my boss's office with a makeshift cushion. Within these rather busy hours of work, in just these two months alone, my mind is already blown with the extreme and regular cases of violence related trauma. I have not felt exhausted, for there is simply no time to be tired.

The first patient I ever saw in clinic was an elderly gentleman with bright blue cataract eyes and a cheeky smile, patiently sitting in the middle of a row of plastic chairs for his turn to be seen. He had a plaster cast on his wrist and as I unassumingly greeted him and pulled out the x-ray from the packet he was holding. To my astonishment, the x-ray revealed his entire wrist joint fragmented into a hundred pieces and shrapnel scattered throughout. "Shot on the way to church a few days ago", he says via a translator, before engaging in light-hearted flirtations with the nursing staff.

This was not an isolated or unique case and on just one Saturday, we operated on a twenty-year-old woman who was attacked by her boyfriend for leaving him after exposing his infidelity. He used a "panga" (extremely large bush knife) to almost take off her left arm at her elbow and her right hand at the wrist. This was followed by a man who was allegedly robbed and shot in both of his feet, followed by another man attacked with a panga. Thereafter, a frightened albino African man presented having been shot in the palm of his hand and lastly a man with a dislocated hip and other injuries following a road traffic accident.

The amount of trauma cases I am witnessing is phenomenal. Although we see a lot of violent crime within the hospital, thankfully I have not witnessed it elsewhere. I have not felt insecure at any point during my stay, although we all hear stories that always keep us vigilant. The hospital has good security, and even a prisoner ward, where incarcerated patients have a hospital bed behind a grilled cell. Reviewing patients here always fills me with uncertainty.

The hospital has all the regular facilities of a general hospital in the UK but laboratory results, notes and x-rays tend to go missing with predictable regularity! The hospital has long open corridors with no walls, connecting departments and wards, providing natural climate control in the stifling heat and a chance to cool down. There are approximately fifteen doctors from the UK working out here, ranging from a professor, UK trained consultants and other junior doctors, like me, in the initial stages of their training. Naturally, it is comforting and easy to build a rapport with so many fellow British doctors, but the hospital is also staffed with locally trained doctors, from various cultures including Afrikaans and Zulu backgrounds. This results in a very friendly, tolerant, diverse workplace.

I am certainly getting a lot of experience and occasionally it feels overwhelming. I suspect my boss realises I do not know anything as he keeps giving me articles and textbooks to read, gradually piling up in my bedroom! I have currently added about one hundred cases to my logbook in these two months, and I can appreciate an overall progression from assisting surgeries to performing the more routine operations with guided supervision.

The vast majority of patients are unable to speak English (thus requiring translations in clinics and on ward rounds), presenting a challenge of communication I have never really faced before. In this regard, the nursing staff are pleasant and very helpful in clinics and in theatre. Although in theatre, the nurses in the morning often greet me happily, say my name and then start giggling amongst each other! I have not quite worked out why yet despite my enquiries!

There is an extremely high prevalence of HIV positive patients in Kwazulunatal, and consequently there is a large caseload of opportunistic infections and tuberculosis. This sadly affects many children and the visits to the paediatric ward often result in mixed feelings for me. The paediatric ward is a single, spacious room with several small beds and cots lined up in multiple rows. Although my patients on this ward are often the energetic, cheeky, charismatic children that have injured themselves playing or falling from mango trees and spend their time in hospital strapped up with their legs or arms dangling in numerous traction devices, I have to walk past newborn babies and older children, suffering from the consequences of HIV, heartbreakingly emaciated and chronically unwell.

On a more uplifting note, all the patients in the hospital have beautiful hymns sung to them daily in Zulu by the nursing staff praying for their healthy recovery. I like to stand quietly on the periphery and enjoy the peaceful singing, relaxing me in the morning in preparation for the inevitable carnage ahead.

Away from work, I live in a small sleepy tourist town on the coast called Mtunzini, approximately thirty kilometres from the hospital. Many of the doctors at the hospital also live here, allowing for regular friendly social activities. The town is quite secluded and very relaxed. Although the level of crime here is not anywhere close to what I witness at the hospital, most houses have intimidating gates and grills on the windows, barbed wire fencing and contracts with private security services. After dark, travelling on foot alone seems unwise.

From my house, I have a beautiful view of a forest and in the nearby horizon, the Indian Ocean. There is a private beach, exclusively for the town residents and before sunset, we often go to play touch rugby or hang out. And after sunset, you can often enjoy miles of endless, sandy beach, all to yourself under a night sky of infinite stars. Within the town, there are number of local amenities, a convenient store that provides all my daily needs, a twenty-four-hour petrol station and a handful of eloquent restaurants.

I have bought a second-hand car, and the morning drive to work takes roughly thirty minutes. As I drive over the undulating hills and past the lush green forestry of Kwazulunatal, I uneasily transport myself from a comfortable, privileged residence, in an affluent area, to my patients, much more impoverished, much more at risk to the dangers of violence and disease than I have ever been or will ever likely to be.

UhambeKahle! (Goodbye in Zulu!)

Saqib.

24.12.2008 – Sabono-aleikum!

Sabono Everyone!

(Sadly, my Zulu vocabulary has not improved much since my last letter!) However, I can now say: Hello. Goodbye. How are you? I am fine. Where's the pain? Does it hurt? Go to the couch. Walk. Bend. Flex. Relax and finally, "Yikes!"

I hope you all are well! Belated Eid Mubarak, and a very early Merry Christmas and Happy New year!

I have now been here three and a half months. Work remains tiring but we are slightly better staffed than when I started and we have a fun group of interns which makes the days very enjoyable and humorous. Three days a week, we have all-day clinics and we are mostly able to finish by four o'clock (I have become a lot more efficient!) but our theatre operating days still continue past six pm, closer seven pm.

I am still learning tremendous amounts and seeing amazing and heart-breaking cases every day. In clinic, we review lots of children with awful deformities that have been neglected by the health systems around them and I often find that the worse the deformity, the sweeter the child and the broader their smile. I have decided to coin this observation, "Noor's Law!"

I am also learning and managing club feet, (a very common paediatric deformity) that can give horrible lifelong walking problems if untreated but can be corrected very easily at birth. It took me a long time to wrap my head around the principle of the treatment, delving into anatomy textbooks and management guidelines. But in the clubfoot clinic, which I now help to run, it is very exciting and rewarding when you see toddlers running around, completely bamboozled why everyone is taking such an interest in them!

We have a middle aged German consultant join the department who has been previously working in arthroscopy

surgery (keyhole surgery) for the past six years.
Understandably, he is very rusty on trauma surgery and so it is
very surreal that I am guiding a senior colleague on performing
femoral nails and skin grafting and other routine operations
here that he has not had much recent exposure to in
Germany!

Memorable cases that I have now witnessed include a male
patient in his mid-twenties that was stabbed in the back to the
hilt with a very large knife. The handle of the knife had come
off but on presentation to the hospital, you could simply see a
very large blade, just to side of the spine, pulsing with regular,
heart-beat movements. The patient was remarkably stable but
immediately taken to the operating room. Of course, they
could not lay the patient on his back for fear of pushing the
blade even further into the heart and the anaesthetist could
not anaesthetise the patient with him lying on his front!

This was when the action began, like clockwork, and as
efficient as a Formula One racing car having its tyres changed
mid-race. Firstly, one doctor pulled out the knife from the
patient's back. Technically speaking, the patient was now
actively bleeding through a huge hole in his heart. Four staff
members then quickly flipped the patient from lying on his
front to lying on his back. The anaesthetist, already prepared,
put the patient asleep and intubated within seconds, whilst
simultaneously the senior surgeon was cracking open the
chest with a mallet and osteotome (and the patient was still
being prepped and draped by another surgeon!). The senior
surgeon quickly got access to the heart, found the hole in the
ventricle and sutured it up. This was all within two minutes
and the surgeon was so confident, he had one of the interns
record the entire procedure on video for teaching purposes.

Another memorable case is of a sweet nine-year-old girl who
has had tuberculosis since the age of three, severely affecting
her spine. Now her neck is curved the wrong way and her
thoracic spine curved the opposite way, so much so her chest
is protruding out miles in front of her and her neck rigid at the
back. She was beginning to have breathing difficulties. There is
nothing we could offer her at this hospital, but she would just

sit, smile and laugh in the clinic. It was deeply sad.

We have had a twenty-one-year-old female and her boyfriend attacked by a psychotic ex-boyfriend – managing to chop off the girl's right hand and the boys left hand whilst severely damaging the boy's right hand too.

There was an eighteen-year-old boy with a tumour in his leg that initially refused hospital treatment, opting for traditional herbal medicine instead. He eventually returned to the hospital with a tumour the size of a rugby ball in his knee, eventually resulting in an amputation above his knee.

I am pleased to report the albino African patient that I operated on after a gunshot to his hand is doing well! Anyhow, there are simply too many stories like this, over and over and over! I am, however, collecting a few of the more interesting cases for my personal memories.

Outside of work, I have just returned from white water rafting in the Tugela River over the weekend. For someone afraid of deep water and swimming, I will admit, it was truly awesome. Firstly, we had to wade into a fast-flowing river (equipped with lifejackets of course) and were shown the technique for gliding down the rapids in case we fell out of the raft! I was petrified as I waded in but all went smoothly and my minimal swimming knowledge came to good use! Then we rafted, hitting rapids followed by calm water, followed by more rapids. The scenery was spectacular, reminiscent of the journey to Dadyal and crossing over the river Jhelum, but rather than go over a rickety suspension bridge, we were on a raft and travelling through the winding rising hills.

And at night we were treated to an amazing lightning show in one of the craziest storms I have ever witnessed and in the morning, just after sunrise we climbed up onto this rock on a hill peak, where we could look out over the land (almost like pride rock in the Lion King) and admire the animals below (mainly Timones and Pumbahs and ostriches!). We all just sat there in relative silence for about 20 minutes admiring the views.

In the past few weekends, I have gotten up at ridiculous o'clock to go whale watching, following hump back whales jumping through the water. I have also seen some hippos and lots of crocodiles with their jaws wide open ready to snap at me. I went 4x4 off road driving with some of the other doctors through a distant forest which was rather dangerous as no one could control the vehicles properly off-road.

I am considering applying for jobs back in the UK, but admittedly, the thoughts of working back at home in orthopaedics is very uninspiring given what I have seen here. I am somewhat compelled to go one stage further and I have contacted a number of international non-governmental organisations to explore other options, including possible emergency work and disaster relief.

It is not all perfect, I am losing a fair amount of weight and it's very hot here, I'm sleeping directly under a fan each night now. I'm getting bitten to pieces by insects which seem to be attracted to insect repellent! Thankfully, malaria is not a major risk here. And of course, a nagging fear for me remains the risks of HIV exposure in the workplace, although the risks are small, it still plays on my mind occasionally. I have had two HIV tests so far just for my own ease of mind, but I think I will regularly get tested out here.

Merry Xmas and a Happy New Year, Sabono-aleikum
Saqib.

05.01.2009 – A Click In My Name!

Dear All,

Happy New Year from sunny South Africa! I hear it's cold in England, snowing in fact - lucky you! I spend my days sweating in the thirty-degree heat and spend the night directly under a whirring ceiling fan whilst listening to the roar of insane thunderstorms. I have now become an expert insect swatter although my ankles still occasionally provide a nutritious feast for some lucky critters! I have not improved my Zulu at all since my last letter, but here is some vocabulary I wish I knew:

Really! Oh my God. You can't be serious? Are you sure? Urrr, I thought that was impossible? That's just insane / gross! This isn't funny anymore! Please, make it stop! Can I sleep now? Does anything work around here?

Also, I feel it is important to note that in the Zulu language, there are three different types of click sounds as part of the spoken language. In writing terms, the clicks are represented by the letters c, x and q. "C" is dental (comparable to a sucking of teeth), "Q" is alveolar (comparable to a bottle top 'pop'), and "X" is lateral (comparable to a click one may do for a walking horse). So my name Sa"Q"ib has a click in it, Sa-(bottle pop)-ib! Perhaps this is what the theatre nurses were laughing at when they pronounced my name. I therefore am proud to refer you to the hilarious Russel Peters Comedy Sketch about African names, "He had a click in his name!" Russel excitedly and comically tells his laughing audience. I too, have a click in my name!

In work related updates, as I was aimlessly wandering past casualty looking for an orthopaedic patient I had been referred, I happened to stumble across a man in a stretcher with what can only be described as a dagger lodged in his head. It was not that one could even see the blade at all, as this was embedded deep into his skull, entering just above the ear, trespassing into the middle of his brain and peeking out through the base of the skull. The handle of the dagger, over 6 inches in length itself, was flush with his skin, demonstrating the sheer aggression required to bury the blade to the hilt. The lack of emotional surprise or reaction from me at this scene demonstrates perhaps the daily exposure to violence is numbing, where it is becoming easier to cope with a shrug than a howl or a tear.

On another Sunday, I got called to the ward by a concerned nurse.

"What do you mean, Sister? Maggots in the wound?" I asked, "Do we use maggots as treatment here for some wounds?" I asked hopefully.

"No, doctor, what do you mean doctor? Come look, doctor", she said.

A very large gentleman had received several operations and also had a central line inserted into his groin (plastic tube into his veins to deliver his antibiotics). And as I peered closer into his groin at a supposedly clean line, one could observe at least ten maggots crawling in and out of his body through the wound and all over his skin! I almost vomited!

I worked on New Year's Day and it went as expected, ridiculously busy! Amongst the cases crashing in included a man accidentally blowing off his hand with a firecracker, a man hit by train, a man hit by car, a man attacked with a panga, a man with his finger bitten off by another man, multiple kids falling out of trees, a man shot in both legs and so it continued. For the first time since I arrived, I truly longed for a simple case, a simple trip on a step, a stumble in the bathroom, a slip on ice.

I am starting to feel like a surgeon now - the increasing experience, the comfort of being in an operating theatre environment, the banter with the scrub nurses, the ability to somehow complete the task, one hardware malfunction or problem after another. I still have much to improve in many facets, but I hope case by case my clinical acumen and technical skills will develop over the next few months. After all, I have only been here four months.

I have been tired and run down over the last few weeks. I am just recovering from a cough and have been unable to sustain a harmonious work life balance. In further bad news, my beloved but rather terrible VW Polo 1.8i Saloon managed to overheat and blow its engine on the way home from a late finish at work. I had not eaten all day and luckily, before breaking down, I had to take a detour to drop off my boss off at his home. I subsequently and thankfully broke down just before the highway and conveniently right outside a KFC Drive thru - where I enjoyed a meal in ironic happiness and blissful KFC contentment!

However, the car requires a major engine repair or perhaps even a suspicious engine replacement. I opted to have it repaired by a local mechanic who appears to the largest Afrikaans man in the world along with his even larger son and daughter. It will cost me over five hundred pounds to repair, which is a valuable amount of possible travel money.

On the brighter side, I am recovering well from my recent illness and I have booked time off at the end of January to continue my travels, wherever they may lead. I wish you all a happy, healthy and peaceful 2009. I have been here long enough now for me to truly miss home!

Sa-"bottle pop"-ib.

02.02.2009 – Die Storie Word Vervolg (Afrikaan - The Story Continues)

Dear All,

I hope you are well and that the New Year has been kind to you so far. Die storie word vervolg is 'Afrikaans' and means the story continues...

Actually, the story is well over half way now and it now feels as though I am soon homeward bound. In one moment, you look over your shoulder to consider all you have seen and achieved in the past few amazing months and the next moment, you look ahead to returning to a place you still call home, where the heart is.

I already have collected some amazing moments and memories here but browsing through my photo archives, I realise I have not really captured the sense of being out here and the wonderful characters I have met and the beautiful places I have visited. And before I know it, the experience is over. For example, it is sad when one of the team members leaves (our German consultant is leaving in a few weeks' time) and it makes you realise how everyone has come together from different parts of the world and at different times in their lives to work in this demanding job and help each other out. Although it seemed initially I was teaching him some operations at one strange stage, it is definitely the other way now as I learn all I can from his experience and expertise!

Regarding work, I will no longer describe the mindless violence as I know it does take its toll and it's not always nice to read about. I will however describe two stories that have been quite moving and quite sad for me, particularly of patients with false hope in what we can achieve as mere doctors.

A young woman in her mid-thirties was unfortunately involved in a road traffic accident. She sustained a dislocation of her cervical spine. Even more unfortunately, she only got to the hospital twenty-four hours later, late at night and by this stage, she had already lost control of her arms, legs and some breathing muscles.

After review, we took her to theatre late at night to try to correct the dislocation with the boss. And although we knew even if we could reduce the dislocation, the spinal cord damage was still likely to be permanent. We battled for three hours to try and get her neck better but in the end, we could not. But the amazing and sad story is the strength and belief this patient showed in us and her courage and patience. For whenever we tried to correct her neck, she was in discomfort but she did not complain and complied with all our instructions bravely. One could see she still believed in what we were doing as she kept trying to see if her arms and legs would miraculously start working after each pull.

And in the end, we failed and decided to try again first thing in the morning with a bigger operation involving open surgery on the neck. That night, we resigned to giving the patient some important breathing exercises but by the morning, she had died.

In another case, a twenty-one-year-old man from Tanzania randomly turned up. He had been referred to us from a small South African hospital, located north, near the border with Mozambique. The patient could not speak Zulu or English, only Swahili, so it boggled me to start with how the patient had made it down this far without being able to explain his situation properly.

After reading a confusing hand written note and some very awkward communications, we managed to work out he had been in a car accident many years ago. He had sustained a severe injury to his shoulder where the bones were broken, along with a big wound and also the nerves to the rest of his arm and hand were badly damaged. He had some initial operations in Tanzania although from the scars, we could not figure out which surgeries had been performed. The result now was that the patient was in severe pain in his upper arm but also his entire lower arm and hand had become irreversibly contracted and wasted, like the thickness of a pencil and quite horrific to see. The surgeons in Tanzania had offered him an amputation but he came to South Africa to fix his hand because this is all he wanted in his life now, a working hand again.

After a long time of further poor communication, we eventually remembered another doctor in a different department could speak Swahili and we enlisted his help. And as soon as the patient could finally express his problems in his own language, one could see the amazing uplifting of his spirit, for he must have been silently frustrated for many days. He spoke of his problems with great hope and passion, pointing to his fingers and describing what had happened in animated detail, so pleased someone could finally understand him.

But in the end, we explained to him that unfortunately it was very unlikely his hand would ever get better and there was very little we could do here, and that brief moment of optimism and positivity just a few seconds earlier came crashing down as his world fell apart again. The young man burst into tears and with his other hand, started hitting himself in the face. It was really sad and emotional just to be in the room. In the end, he decided he would travel back to Tanzania to have an amputation but only after the Swahili speaking doctor consoled him and shared a cigarette.

There are happier moments at work. By far my favourite part of the job has been the children. One of my colleagues argues here that African kids are the cutest all over the world and although I initially argued that all children are cute, these smiling, adorable patients really have grown on me. In clinic, it's such a shame they are only seen for five minutes after a long wait in the queue, and often travelling many hours to arrive, sometimes leaving their homes at three or four o'clock in the morning and travelling the same long distance on the journey home. I have now bought an almost endless supply of lollipops to hand out to them for their reward of waiting to see us and it does work very well sometimes to my advantage.

The initially tired and grumpy kids, who are happy on their moms' laps, but reluctant to show us how well they are walking, now all of a sudden are up and tottering to the other side of the room in pursuit of a strange doctor waving a lollipop. And the children who have had operations on their arms and do not want to move are desperately reaching into the air for the lollipops, trying to scramble them off me! The lollipops are also useful to bribe the nurses at the end of the clinic who all get annoyed unless they get their 'pop' fix!

I have not achieved much out of work, but some reflective time enjoying the beach and the surrounding areas. My car that I fixed has subsequently broken down again so I am still without a car. Having said that, most of the doctors' cars right now all seem to be breaking down, it is related to the weather they say as it is scorching, regularly hitting thirty to forty degrees Celsius!

I have also visited the Apartheid museum in Johannesburg. This is a humbling, moving experience demonstrating South Africa's darker days. It describes how apartheid developed and the humiliation and atrocities endured by the indigenous people under a racist regime. It describes the enormous strife and suffering which led to the unity of brave people and how they struggled and battled to achieve equality. The museum showcases a collection of amazing videos, footage of tens of thousands of unarmed protesters running in unison down a street or dancing and singing in front of armed soldiers. The museum's message ends with a new era of hope, of equality and justice to all.

I have now started applying for posts back in snowy England. It is unlikely I will be successful in obtaining an orthopaedic training contract but with what I have achieved here, I would not change my experience for the world. I have become a better doctor and person since being here, and I am simply hopeful of being offered a short term six-month post so I can settle for a little while before considering bigger challenges.

I have also been asked to write for a UK medical journal of my experiences here so hopefully when I write it, I can put all my words into a more vivid and inspirational description for you all to read.

I leave you with a phrase that Nelson Mandela quoted during

his inaugural speech, 1994:

"Let there be justice for all. Let there be peace for all. Let there be work, bread, water and salt for all. Let each know that for each, the body, the mind and the soul have been freed to fulfil themselves. Never, never and never again shall it be that this beautiful land will again experience the oppression of one by another and suffer the indignity of being the skunk of the world. Let freedom reign.

The sun shall never set on so glorious a human achievement!

God bless Africa!"

Saqib

23.03.2009 – Ubenosuku Oluhle Lomama (Happy Mother's Day)

Dearest All,

Ubenosuku Oluhle Lomama (Happy Mother's Day) – translated kindly by Muzi, the plaster room chief! I hope you are all well and happy. I continue with my ramblings, seven months into South Africa, with some deeper thoughts and the learning of my journey.

The last 24 hours summarises my experience in South Africa so far and the country itself.

Late last night, whilst on a typical twenty-four-hour call, I operated on a sick child with a septic (infected) knee, having to drain a lot of pus from inside his knee joint. This was followed by a young man who had been hit by a car, breaking both his legs, with a significant open fracture (bone exposed out the skin) on one side. And by 2am, his wounds were cleaned and the three fractures were stabilised, two with external fixators (metal frames on the outside of his leg). This was followed by an uncomfortable night on the floor in stifling heat (as all the beds were taken) whilst also being intermittently called to the emergency room for orthopaedic problems. And I was up again at seven-thirty in the morning, just in time for a quick shower before another morning teaching session. Thereafter, I settled into the all-day clinic. Here I sleepily battled through the morning patients, discharging as many patients as I possibly could and handing out the occasional lollipop to a bored child and sneaking one for myself whilst glugging on a can of coke purchased from the 'sandwich lady'.

And in the afternoon off work (given to you if you have worked the previous twenty-four-hour shift), I visited an orphanage that I have recently volunteered at. The orphanage is built on church land, with a glorious view of the hills of Zululand in the backdrop and the blazing African sun shining through. I clumsily played with five children who had lost their families to HIV. I pushed a two-year-old on a swing who knew exactly how she wanted to be pushed and I struggled to feed a ten-month-old sweet potato mash. If I did not fill the spoon quickly enough, she would happily put her face quickly into the entire bowl! And I held onto a six-month-old already facing the horrible complications of HIV infection.

As it approached sunset, I drove to the beach and played rugby with fifteen others as the sun set over land. I engaged in conversation with another medic without realising the rest around us had dispersed. And as the epic conversation ensued, dusk turned to darkness and the beach became empty. And the stars popped out one by one by one.

Arriving home, I reluctantly enjoyed the most basic of my own cooking as I dreamt of home cooked food. And I settled for a night outside, loading up on insect repellent as I swung in a hammock, trying again to count the stars, getting to two hundred and sixty-seven before more appeared, others disappeared and others shot across the sky.

I trudged inside, sipped on my dwindling supply of apple juice and wrote out the following thoughts.

Healing: it is not about the right surgery, it is about the right words

I have now been involved in easily over 300 operations. I am now comfortable with all but the severest orthopaedic emergencies. I am a vastly different surgeon to the inexperienced doctor that first came out here. I greet the theatre team in the morning with hopeful enthusiasm that we may finish on time, knowing the responsibility is on me as it is my operating list. I help wheel the patients in. I set up the operating table with all the necessary add-ons. I teach the juniors what I know of the operation.

I help transfer the patient across and then position the patient how I want. I ask the theatre staff to set up how I want. I think about the operation, how it will start, how it will progress, how it will finish. I prepare the patient, position my drapes. I battle through faulty equipment and unforeseen problems. I battle through difficult operations, solving some problems, calling senior help if I cannot. I banter with the anaesthetist throughout the operation if things are going well. I banter with the anaesthetist a little less if things are not going so well. I ask for the radio to be turned on always.

I finish the operation and transfer the patient off the table, I write the operation note, and I write my post-operative plans. I get ready for the next patient. And at the end of the operating list, I thank the theatre staff for the arduous work of the day and I apologise to all for finishing later then I had hoped. And at the end of the working day, I feel I really know what it is to be a surgeon.

Yet, without the words to communicate with the patient, the effort I fear is meaningless. Despite the translators, I fear one has lost his greatest healing tool. There can be no adequate words of encouragement. There can be no reassurances. There can be no serious explanations of expectations. One cannot describe how the operation went. And a surgeon's most useful instrument, that of the tongue, is tied because a smile or thumbs up can only go so far when talking to a worried patient.

And as we follow the patients up, knowing they do not fully understand and that we do not have the time to translate and explain perfectly, one sees the frustrations between both doctor and patient. One sees unhappiness that could have been avoided, no matter what the surgery and how well it went.

Between any human relation, whether is a patient, an acquaintance or a loved one, I have learnt the right words can give hope. The right words can give comfort. The right words can give pain relief. The right words can heal the most. And so, never take your words for granted, to whom you are speaking to, because when it is not said or lost in translation, it is never the same. And a kind word to another human can make the necessary difference in life. And I believe it is more powerful than surgery, I have learnt that. Do not be afraid to communicate when you need to and more importantly, do not be afraid to communicate even if you don't need to.

Of life's risks and its fragility

By all accounts, the last few months have been difficult. Our house was broken into last month, despite the alarms going off. Thankfully no one was inside to get hurt and thankfully nothing valuable of mine was stolen but sadly my two housemates have had their laptops taken. Since then, we have had a new super sensitive alarm system installed but frustratingly, the alarm can go off regularly through the night and one can never be sure if it is a false alarm or if an intruder truly is outside.

Furthermore, earlier this month, I had my first occupational exposure to HIV infected blood after a minor eye splash. Although the risk is negligible, I was started on anti-retroviral therapy to make the negligible risk even more miniscule. And within a day, I was battling the side-effects of the therapy with severe nausea, vomiting and blistering headaches. The anti-sickness tablets became more and more ineffective and I spent the days very drowsy. I lasted ten days of the twenty-eight day course before I could no longer continue if I wanted to function properly.

And I realise with these two events and with all life's events, we are always at risk with what we do and the essence of life itself is very delicate, for it only takes one moment for it to change forever. But all our actions in life carry a risk and in life, one must still live. I have learnt our lives are fragile and therefore they are precious. I have learnt your life and those of the ones you love must be cherished, as one just never knows when it may change.

The God of all people

As I gaze out at a million stars and beyond, knowing we are a tiny fragment of the universe, I think of the many people I have met and seen along this journey. And I realise, being so small and insignificant, just how similar as people we all really are. I see the five-year-old girl holding tightly onto her seven-year-old brother's hand as they trespass on the long road to school, putting her trust in him. I see the mother holding her child and whispering "Thula, thula, thula" as her baby cries (meaning "hush, hush, hush"). I watch as the old ladies working at the checkout at the supermarket gossip happily whilst the younger worker looks bored as she sends an SMS from her phone. I interrupt animated theatre staff to ask them why they speak so frantically and they describe troubles with their husbands, or that their teenage daughter used the wrong washing up powder and how children are difficult to manage. I hear the nurses sing beautiful hymns to their patients and I hear patients listening to the same hymns on their radios, whilst they sit in clinic. And I too, find the beautiful Zulu Christian hymns so soothing.

With all these characters I have met, I see the same patterns and no matter what our culture, background, religion or language, we are the same as human beings, with the same longings and yearnings in our hearts. And our hearts are all equal and all God given, from the God of all religions, the God of all people. We all have the same needs and we all have the same problems. We all seek love, we seek belonging, we seek comfort, we seek support and we seek guidance. We all laugh at the same things. And we all cry at the same things. And we are equal. And may God bless us all.

Ubenosuku Oluhle Lomama (Happy Mother's Day)

As I have held a child and played with children that now may never have that pure blessing of a mother's love, I feel it fitting to end on a tribute to all mothers, on Mother's Day.

For my mother, who has given me everything I have ever asked for – Giyabonga (I thank you). For all mothers, those that are dearly departed, for those mothers in the present, old and new, and to all those mothers who will be in the future, for filling the world with its purest form of love and happiness – Siyabonga (We thank you).

And to all those who may have been blessed by God to have found a love in their life even half as much as their mothers , and been fortunate enough to hold onto it, may you always treasure it and never forget its worth.

Giyabonga Gokulu (I thank you very much)
Sakhile (my Zulu name!)

21.05.2009 – Rambling Stories

Dearest All,

I write the penultimate chapter of this journey. I am soon to return to England and in a single week's time I will be packing my bags and begin travelling homeward bound. I have truly experienced what I have wanted to experience, seen all I had hoped to see.

I have already written out my final chapter of words and thoughts but I shall send them in a few days when I start packing my bags. For now, I am afraid there are a few more stories to tell before I go.

These last two months have proven to be very busy in travel. I have visited Zimbabwe, Namibia, Cape Town, Swansea and Cuba, but firstly, an update from my last letter.

The HIV test

I described an incident of sustaining an eye splash exposure to infected blood, commencing anti-retroviral therapy, followed by vomiting, severe headaches, the inability to complete my course of therapy and the anxious wait for a blood test.

The time for the test came and I was counselled about the HIV test by the nurse. She proceeded to prick my finger and squeeze my blood onto the two test strips in front of her. And naturally one begins to worry about the possible outcome - the chances are miniscule, the implications, however enormous. And as I sweated, eyes glued to the test strips, the nurse calmly pulled out a catalogue of African furniture and bed linen, asking me if I would consider buying them as presents for family in the UK. Hardly the most appropriate timing, I thought to myself, but as I admired some of Africa's finest embroidery and haggled prices, I was happily told the test was negative. To celebrate, I put in an order for some very expensive table cloths but changed my mind soon after.

27

Victoria Falls smuggling

It was a lifelong dream to visit the Victoria Falls, to stand in its very presence and be inspired by the power of nature and magnificent beauty. I managed to fulfil this ambition, standing in front of the falls, arms aloft and becoming drenched by the hail that the waterfall rains onto its admirers. For a second perspective, I also jumped off the Victoria Falls Bridge and swung on a bungee towards a river gorge, enjoying the view upside down with adrenaline flowing through my veins. And for a final perspective, I flew above the falls in a flimsy micro-light machine (like a tiny helicopter) and gawped at the stunning views from above.

But it was not the waterfalls that inspired me the most. It was the people of Zimbabwe and their stories, each one as simple as it was heart-breaking. Along my journey, I met and spoke to many wonderful characters. I felt at peace talking with them and even late into the dark evening, I felt safe amongst strangers, walking alongside their travel home and listening to their stories. There is no fear of violence like the heartlands of South Africa. There are no guns on display or hidden knives. The constant curtain of apprehension hanging over me whilst in South Africa was lifted for a few carefree nights.

Although there are too many stories to tell, I recall one elderly lady who walked back with me from Zambia to Zimbabwe, an approximate five kilometres walk and over the Victoria Falls Bridge. She had travelled many miles to visit her sister in a Zambian hospital, who had been involved in a car accident. She motioned chopping signals at her arm and leg to explain to me the injuries sustained but I was not sure if she was describing broken bones or amputations.

When we got to the Zimbabwean border, she suddenly stopped and hid in the trees. I wondered if she knew another secret route across the border, but she was simply placing some banned face cream in her underwear in order to smuggle it across. When we got out onto the other side, she giggled away, putting her prized possession back into her bag, but not before describing the virtues of this magical cream. Soon after, she realised she would be missing the only train back to her home. She lifted her skirt, said goodbye and ran like old ladies do, with efficient, careful steps, into the distance, shouting "God bless you Noah (Noor?)" for the $2 I gave for her train fare.

A hot air balloon over shanty towns

Namibia has the second lowest population density in the world and south of Windhoek (the country's capital city), there is only a population of 150,000 in an area four times the size of the UK. And so as soon I landed, I hired a 4x4 from the airport and ventured southward, in search of emptiness and the solitude of a new scene I had not witnessed, the African desert. I drove along dusty gravel roads, through a mountain hill pass with steep drops, no barriers and breath-taking views. One could drive for over an hour and not see another vehicle or fellow human until another vehicle perhaps comes trailing through in the opposite direction. It is customary, it seems, to nod your head or wave at the opposite driver, just to say, "I acknowledge and accept your presence in this deserted beautiful country".

As you follow the dusty tracks of previous vehicles that have passed before you, you would see the tyre imprints swerving from side to side, racing uncontrollably towards the sides of the road and then suddenly veering back towards the middle. As regularly as this happened, it was possible to imagine that very vehicle in front of you moving in different directions and you could not help but smile. I did at one stage, get out of the car, just to see my own tyre tracks, saw that they were straighter than others, and proudly jumped back in.

The Namibian desert is red and the dunes are the largest in the world. The curves and the patterns they create, rising up with the background of clear blue skies, are mesmeric. The showpiece in the desert is Dead Vlei, a terrace of white clay in the middle of the dunes where dead black trees scatter, in a constellation of shapes, standing proudly, over 900 years old in death, as if paying tribute to time itself.

I rose into the skies in a hot air balloon over the desert to watch the sunrise. Floating, drifting silently through the air, gazing into the desert, the mountains and the changing colours of the sky, I serenely accepted that the world truly is magically beautiful. At the end of the ride, I was given a postcard of the balloon flying above the dunes, saying "Dream it... or live it" and I have decided to keep the postcard.

On the way back to the airport, I picked up hitchhikers for the very first time in my life although in South Africa we were strictly warned not to. However, in this country, it seemed rude not too, being the only car driving in my direction for miles. Two men, pushing a goat cart up a hill seemed to need to go somewhere. They sat silently at the back of the car and as I tried to make conversation, I did not get far. A few yes's and no's followed by silence. Perhaps it is the isolated nature of the country that its people were not natural talkers or perhaps, I too had been stunned into silence by its very isolated nature.

And then in the scorching midday sun, another figure, a young woman flagged me down. She was carrying her baby and was visiting her grandma in the next town. Once again, the conversation was minimal, so I gave her my water bottle and peanut snack bar, and 80km later and a little out of my way, I dropped her off by her house, in a shanty town of dozens of one-room shacks, made up of just metal sheets and wood. And I was reminded again, that despite its glorious, gorgeous scenery, I was still in Africa.

A toothless grin from the Rainbow City

I was lucky enough to be invited to a paid trip to Cape Town by Smith & Nephew for an Orthopaedic course. However, I managed to miss my outgoing flight, a sickening first for me, sitting forlorn and dejected, bags packed in the airport lounge. Luckily, I made it to Cape Town at midnight on the next available flight. Cape Town itself is a phenomenal city. As I stood on the balcony of my hotel, I was confused. I simply did not know in which direction to gaze, for looking outwards, I saw the city, the Atlantic Ocean and the boats that passed into the harbour. But turning to the right, I would gaze at the towering Table Mountain, guarding the city like an ancient sentry on duty. After a cable car ride to the top of the mountain, I had a panoramic view of the city and from a distance, I gazed upon Robben Island, the prison that incarcerated men that would end up changing the world. In the evening, I drove up to a parking bay and looked down onto the twinkling city lights.

The city is rich and vibrant. The weather, despite the winds, is mostly very favourable and I was treated to four days of perfect sunshine even in its wintertime. The people are diverse and happy. They live and work together, races, religions and cultures. I wandered through the Jewish quarter and the Malay quarter. There are numerous restaurants of unique blends of foods, catering for every appetite.

It was Nelson Mandela himself that described 'a rainbow nation at peace with itself and the world' but it was when a toothless taxi driver grinned and talked proudly of the rainbow nation, that I truly believed it existed in Cape Town.

Nice suits and nice canteens

I have travelled to Swansea for a job interview. From South Africa to Wales was certainly a culture shock and a big bump back to the NHS. It was strange to wear a suit as I have become used to wearing my sandals and T-shirts to work. It was odd to sit in a dedicated hospital canteen and hospital food never smelt so nice. It was bizarre not to see queues of haphazard patients, stretched across corridors. And it was awkward to be back.

A sweet old lady spilled coffee onto my suit in the canteen and my jacket was wiped down by a frantic volunteer describing what a nice suit it was in a high-pitched Welsh accent. Pleased about the compliment, I had a feeling it would be a good day.

And indeed, I have been offered the job and I start in July. The work entails trauma surgery research, orthopaedic teaching of medical students and some clinical work. I suspect it will be nothing compared to where I have been, adjusting will take some energy.

You snooze, you lose

It's true, I have not been to Cuba but an orthopaedic surgeon from Cuba has recently joined our team. He is a jolly man in his fifties with an affectionate, crooked smile. Over the years, he has worked in Cuba, in Angola and in South Africa. His story is an inspiring one to me. He tells me of his life's story. He has been happily married to his wife for 27 years but it took him over a year to find the courage to speak to her as they travelled on the same Cuban bus together. He tells me of his battles with a major illness as a young man (the details I will not go into) but how he survived against all the odds and when he recovered, continued his training in Orthopaedic surgery with even more determination.

And he tells me, that as a head of an entire surgical department in a Cuban hospital, his wages were $30/month. His reason to work in South Africa is purely a financial one, leaving his parents and family to earn a living. He earns approximately the same wage as I do, but half of it is paid in taxes to the Cuban government. He lives in austere hospital accommodation with his wife in comparison to my idyllic Mtunzini dwelling.

And even into his fifties, he is working the same twenty-four hour shifts I do. Yet he is happy and enthusiastic. He is a wonderful joke and story teller, in a mixture of Spanish, English and Zulu. He is a brightness to the department and a spark of energy to the daily grind. "You snooze, you lose" in Zulu he shouts from the clinic room to the next patient in the queue. Listening to his story, I am truly privileged to have the career I have and the wages I earn. For here, in South Africa, I am earning a third of my UK wage but here is a man with more qualifications, more dedication, more experience, with more commitment, thousands of miles away from home, happy with his situation. He promised when he returns to Cuba and is rich and retired, I am invited to visit. And with his story, I too am determined to succeed in this career.

I hope to see you all soon.
Saqib.

25.06.2009 – The Journey Home

Dear all,

This is my last letter from South Africa, which reflects all I have seen and learnt during the past ten months. I would like to thank you all for reading and tolerating my spam over the last year! I write this from the airport, as I wait to board and fly northwards, away from this captivating land.

I have travelled a thousand miles from home. And I have learnt so much.

I have seen a man with a large knife penetrating his skull and exiting the other side, still breathing.

I have seen a man shot 6 times and not sustain a single significant injury.

I have seen a woman who has lost her hands at the hands of violence.

I have seen a newborn baby that has been shot and lost his arm.

I have witnessed the destructive force of man's fear, man's greed, man's anger and man's jealousy.

I have seen a child with a severe spinal deformity and the sweetest smile.

I have held a child in my arms that is suffering from the consequences of AIDS.

I have realised how people's lives can change forever in a moment of illness or accident. But also, how other lives are changed from the moment they were born.

And I have never worked so hard, in the days and deep into the nights. I have been educated by brave people. I have hoped I made a difference.

I have done honourable deeds. But I have also made mistakes and felt their burdens weigh down on me. I have truly felt like a surgeon.

I have watched the bluest waves and the greenest waves of the clearest oceans, lashing to the horizon and back again.

I have drifted in a hot-air balloon over a desert and mountains, soaring over the skies, watching as the sky turned from a darkness, to a purplish, to a pinkish, to an orangish, to a yellowish to a bright blue sky and a majestic sun shining through.

And I have stood barefoot on an empty flawless beach, looking into the distance as the sky turned from a sapphire blue to a lavender pink, a crimson red, an indigo violet and into a black night studded with white lights.

And I have sat silently, gazing up at this night sky, counting endless and uncountable sparkling stars as they greet me one by one, palpating the infinity of the universe beyond and accepting my place in it.

I have crashed through waves on a speeding boat, chasing whales migrating to their destination.

I have walked with lions who shared their travels with me and their passion and strength.

I have seen crocodiles, hippos, rhinos, giraffes, zebras, elephants, buffalos, eagles, and the elegance in all of life's creatures.

I have felt the solitude of the endless burning desert, of sand dunes that rise and fall in perfect symmetry.

I have paddled through river rapids and drifted through calmer waters only to battle through more rapids that awaited me.

I have stood in front of a glorious waterfall and being soaked by its smoking thunder. And I have flown above this waterfall, watching the energy of nature run through its canyons and gorges as I blew in the winds above.

I have jumped from a bridge and felt the speed of the world beneath me, above me and running through me as I fell manically towards the earth. I then swung upside down and laughed.

I have gazed upon a setting sun as it descends through the peaks of unending mountains that will never change their position.

I have admired bright city lights at dusk from a higher place, watching the activity and hustle of our daily and nightly lives.

I have heard nurses sing prayers in unison, for the blessings of their patients.

I have been in the company of brave people, learning their stories and have been humbled. I have been inspired by people, who remain strong with hope despite nothing else.

I have worked with dedicated volunteers who have sacrificed for a greater good and their beliefs.

I have been in awe of an island that was once a prison, where a few good men's sacrifice proved the world they were wrong.

And above all, I have seen God's most beautiful creation and smiled at her. And have been graced by God to see her smiling back. And lose it again.

I have been enlightened. I feel God in all His people and in their goodness and kindness. And that we are all equal. And that we all have the same beating heart and the same red blood running through it, no matter our colour, or our culture or our religion. I have met different people, but have only seen one world.

I have felt that those boundaries of race, colour, religion, language and creed are only created in man's mind but not in his spirit and I have seen that the spirit can still triumph.

I have truly held the finest treasure of the world in my hands. But have also watched it slip through my fingers as I tried to hold on.

And now I begin the journey home, I return a humbled man, a gentler man and a poorer man for all I have seen, all I have won and all I have lost.

With my final words, I thank you all for allowing me to walk my awkward steps with you along your very own journeys.

May God bless you always.
Saqib

Haiti (2010)

On the 12th January 2010, a devastating earthquake with a catastrophic magnitude struck twenty-five kilometres west of Port-au-Prince, the capital city of Haiti. Although the official death toll varies widely, many reports suggest that over 100,000 people lost their lives in the immediate aftermath. Heart-breaking imagery from the destruction was widespread throughout all media formats and an emergency international relief response was haphazardly being coordinated, partly due to the sudden loss of government infrastructure within Haiti itself.

At the time, I was working in Swansea as a tutor for the MSc in Trauma Surgery and was still somewhat settling back into the UK. Although I remember numerous appeals for medical assistance from non-governmental organisations and browsing related forums and message-boards in relation to this, I do not recall clamouring to volunteer as a medical professional with any grandiose vigour. I completed some initial online enquiries, all but forgot about them and continued at my work.

However, in late January, I was contacted by the Haiti Hospital Appeal, a London based charity via an internet form I must have completed. They were requesting medical personnel to assist as they had started accepting earthquake victims in their facility. The details were extremely sparse and I was very apprehensive about the request. However, after researching the organisation, it became apparent they were an established presence in Haiti many years before the earthquake, many years before the world, other aid organisations, the media or celebrities cared. It was this fact alone that gave the organisation the credibility I needed to trust in their project. I believed with all my heart they would also be a presence in Haiti long after the earthquake, when the world would have simply forgotten again.

My work at the time did not involve significant clinical responsibilities, and so I was able to negotiate time off work at short notice to travel.

11.02.2010 – We Are Boarding Now

Dear Family, Friends, Colleagues, Readers and Bloggers,

I am currently writing on my mobile phone from Gatwick Airport, London, ready to board a flight with a team in support of the recent earthquake in Haiti.

I am travelling for two weeks to a hospital that was established by a British charity even before the January earthquake. The hospital is based in Cap-Haitien, five or six hours north of Port-au-Prince. I understand the facilities are very basic but since the earthquake, the hospital has started accepting casualties from the epicentre. There are stories of crushed spines, children with amputations, large pressure sores and much more. Currently, I appear to be the only medic on the team at the airport.

A wise person recently taught me that there is no such thing as true altruism and if I am truly honest, there are also a few personal reasons for my journey. However, with these two hands, I hope perhaps I can contribute somewhat to the effort. I am acutely aware of my own limitations in both ability and experience. I know I do not offer much. I also know the way the world endlessly rotates on its axis and Haiti will continue to spin whether I am there or not. For those worried about my nomadic nature, please do not fear, my feet are still firmly on the ground and I remain focussed on my longer-term goals too.

If you did read my diaries in Africa, you will remember it took me ten months to realise that the most important tool for any doctor is not medical knowledge, surgical ability or hospital facilities but the ability to communicate. It is language that holds the key to inspire, comfort and give hope. Watching a foreigner attempt a new language always make a local person smile and giggle. Being able to comfort or educate a patient with simple words offers more than any intervention. What good is the operation if the patient does not know what was done and what to expect?

Haitian Creole is the spoken language of Haiti although French is the official language. Creole, although regarded as an independent language, has a significant French influence and therefore I am hopeful to grasp the basics as I still remember a few smatterings of French from my school days. I will now be trading those hard Zulu phrases I barely learnt in twelve months (all ten of them!) - Sabona (hello). Sawabonga (Thank you). Unjani? (how are you?). Sapele (I am fine). Yeahbo (yes). Xa (No). Gobisa and xondise (flex and extend) and pagamisa um lens (lift your leg in the air!) for my new language of Creole. Bonswa (Good evening). Wi (Yes). Non (No) and eske ou kabkanpe? (Can you stand up?).

I would like to thank my family for offering their unlimited support and my boss at work for granting me the sudden time off. Also thank you to Ceri and Geraldine (your baby pram and cot are on the plane!), to my brother for his medical donations and my mom for her endless supply of paracetamol to the hospital!

Surgical consultants at my workplace in Swansea have already approached me, interested in the possibility of sending out regular surgical teams from Swansea, ultimately far more qualified persons than myself. I am hopeful I will be able to establish connections in Haiti for such visits to be possible!

For everyone else, I will send a link for any donations and support you may want to give. If not, I would be grateful for your prayers or well wishes, to whichever God you do or do not pray to, for they are all important to me. Please hope for the well-being of the Haitian people and the health and safety of the team I am travelling with and for their safe return. If we do lose communication, those who know me best will know that wherever I am in the world, near or far, the last thought on my mind and in my heart before I fall asleep each night will be of those people in the world I love the most - you all know who you are.

We are boarding now. With love always,

Saqib.

12.02.2010 – Five One Pound Coins

Dear Readers,

The last 24 hours have been frenziedly hectic. I am currently in Santiago in the Dominican Republic. I shall briefly describe the journey so far.

After frantically packing and organising, I fell asleep in my bed in Birmingham at midnight and woke up at two a.m. to drive to Kent. There, I met the organiser of this mission at five a.m., parked my car at his house and then to Gatwick airport for a team briefing at an airport hotel.

The hotel room was already crammed full of boxes with random assortments of donated medical supplies. I sleepily met the other three volunteers who would be my companions on this journey. However, before we had time to become acquainted and get comfortable, we were asked to start packing medical kit from the boxes that we thought may be useful. We only had three empty suitcases as spare luggage to pack into. After fifteen minutes of curiously opening boxes to see what goodies were inside, I started laughing. I imagined one of those artificial team building role play exercises that I would often smirk at in the past. I imagined sitting around a table with a scrap of paper that read:

"You have had two hours' sleep. You are travelling to a Haitian hospital with a nurse, a physio and journalist whom you have only just met. You are at the airport and must choose which medical supplies to take. You have between fifteen and fifty patients and you do not know what facilities the hospital has. Discuss amongst your team and make an appropriate list."

We all agreed on an eclectic assortment of antibiotics, analgesics, dressings and gloves. Being from a surgical background, I sneaked in sutures, sterile blades and some ridiculous looking surgical instruments I had never seen before!

After a briefing we were given Haiti Hospital Appeal T-shirts and rolled on through the airport with a barrage of awkwardly packed luggage.

The flight was unremarkable but inspiringly at Gatwick airport, four or five random passers-by would read our T-shirts, wish us luck and some would give donations. One little girl came with her mother and said she wanted to help as she handed over her five one pound coins.

We arrived at Peurto Plata and had a little explaining to do as the customs officers opened our baggage filled to the brim with medications. A few simple gestures pointing to our T-shirts and saying Haiti soon got us through with no worries.

From here we travelled two hours to Santiago and met one of the founders of the charity, who has explained the work so far. I now have a much greater understanding of the hospital itself and its scope of work. It truly is a remarkable story in its own right. I will describe it in my next post along with an insight into my new team and the job at hand.

Today we travel across the border into Haiti and to Cap-Haitien, a city largely unaffected by the earthquake directly. It is only then will we get a feel for the country and its current problems. It is a five-hour bus journey. Today is a national day of mourning in Haiti for the earthquake victims.

With love always,

Saqib

13.02.2010 – The Hospital That Actors Built (No, Not George Clooney!)

Dear Readers,

After another gruelling day of travel and endless waiting, whilst simultaneously admiring both the Dominican Republic and Haitian landscape, our team has arrived at our destination. I write this on my phone at 4am local time, hidden under a mosquito net as a cockerel cockle-doodle-doos outside. I suspect this maybe the best or even the only time I will have freedom to write my thoughts to you all.

Although we have not been to the ward yet or seen patients, hearing now direct first-hand accounts of Haitians affected by the earthquake and the verbal reports from the volunteer team already out here, the situation has suddenly become all too real. I am not sure I can grasp or understand the sheer scale of the disaster. Already the stories I have learnt are tragic beyond words I could ever describe. Haitians are stoic, hardened people and when a local hospital volunteer, working as a translator, began to tell of the situation, towards the end of a horrific description, you could hear his voice breaking in two and see the tears behind his eyes. For now though, on Valentines weekend, I will not recall these stories until after Sunday for fear of breaking any of your hearts on a weekend dedicated to love and romance.

Instead, I shall tell you of a hopeful, inspiring story, the one about a hospital built by actors (no, not George Clooney!).

Although I may have the specifics somewhat wrong, I hope you will get the picture.

In 2005, two 'out of work' British actors, aged 22, from Kent attended a Christian event dedicated to the concept of justice. At the end of the event, upon a notice board they saw a request for accommodation from a Haitian pastor who was visiting the UK. They duly obliged and gave their number to the pastor that they could offer a room whenever he arrived.

The pastor arrived in the UK, but firstly went to a conference in Birmingham dedicated to third world action and support. The pastor told of the healthcare problems in Haiti and pitched a request for support for a hospital in Haiti to all the aid organisations at the conference. However, he did not receive any interest. Saddened and without much money, he called those actors from the church who had offered him accommodation and made his way to Kent for somewhere to stay.

Once he arrived, he told his hosts of what he was trying to do and how he did not find any support from any of the NGOs. The actors looked at each other, looked at the pastor and said they would help.

A few months later they visited Haiti and were appalled by what they saw, with a massive maternal and neonatal mortality rate and dire healthcare. Soon after, the Hospital Haiti Appeal was founded, by two actors and their friends who had no experience in this field, no logistical, administrative, local or medical knowledge. However, they did have a heart and determination to help the Haitian people and thus far, their work has been remarkable.

Despite obvious numerous setbacks including bouts of regular hurricanes, in 2007, a health clinic was opened for free care to the local people. From there, they also established a children's centre specifically to help disabled children (in which I am staying now in a side annex). And in 2009, they began work on the ultimate goal, a purpose built maternity and paediatric unit for the people of Cap-Haitien run by the people of Cap-Haitien.

Now before I round off the story, I am still inspired and finding it difficult to imagine how three to four young friends from Britain with little expertise dropped everything for this exceptionally difficult project so far away, long before the earthquake and the media attention on the country. Having now met one of the British founders (who has lived here for a year in exceptionally humble dwellings) and seen how hard they are working, I can already say these are amazing people.

The maternity unit building was almost complete a month ago when the earthquake hit. Since then the organisation has worked around the clock to complete as many buildings as possible and change their direction temporarily from maternity to assist the injured patients.

The patients from Port au Prince have been sent north to the local government hospitals here and more patients are waiting to be offloaded from the US medical ships (remember there are estimated 300,000 people injured - every hospital, clinic and facility is swamped in the entire country).

A well-established Catholic hospital nearby has constructed eight field tents on its grounds and each tent already has one hundred patients. Within each tent are numerous patients from the earthquake, sustaining major injuries to their limbs and spines, including many adults and children who have had amputations.

The Haiti Hospital Appeal project has now started taking some of the spinal patients and is gearing up for more admissions. Surgeons from the USA have already briefly visited the hospital and completed minor operations here and we are expecting a team of medical personnel from the US (including general and orthopaedic surgeons) this weekend for some more activity on site (although what exactly is unclear yet).

I will write again about the hospital itself tomorrow and the needs of the patients here and at the tented hospital, which I also hope to visit.

With love,
Saqib

14.02.2010 – A Valentine's Message From Haiti

Dear Readers,

Tonight, on the eve of Valentine's Day, I really tried to look for heart-warming and uplifting stories from Haiti before beginning the tales of sadness and heartache later in these updates.

However the only romance I have found for you is that tonight as I write this, above this disaster-stricken country is the most phenomenal theatre of glittering and twinkling stars that outshine even the truly amazing night scenes I saw in Africa.

Today I did my first day's work in what probably appears to be Haiti's first ever dedicated spinal and rehab unit - an incompletely built building with three different sized rooms and a corridor connecting them. This had been the maternity unit 'to-be' with one of the rooms designed to be an operating theatre (by that I mean it has white tiles on the walls rather than nothing!). In each of these overflowing rooms now are patients injured from the earthquake.

Surrounding the incomplete 'maternity ward' is the hastily started 'paediatric' ward which workmen are constructing tirelessly (and I mean tirelessly!) to have completed in a few days' time to start taking more spinal patients.

An accident and emergency nurse from the UK who has been with the charity for two weeks (and has been busy in Port Au Prince for a week of that) has been crucial in implementing the medical aspect of the care of these patients. I could write an entire post on her alone but already in my first forty-eight hours I have met such wonderful and remarkable people, I ought to write an entire post titled 'Heroes' soon.

As we walked into the building, we were met with an unparalleled sense of joy, not only from the hospital staff but from beaming, singing and laughing patients.

And then we met the patients and heard their stories with a medical hand over. This is what we heard 15 times:

'Crushed spine. Paraplegic. Massive pressure sores'

Myself and the physiotherapist then went around on a much longer ward round to start looking at each patient individually. We spoke to each patient, examining them and scouring the notes (or collection of scribbles on papers). It was a baffling experience as the notes would alternate between French, English, Swedish, German, and there was even an entry from the Russian emergency air ambulance service!

These patients have many remarkable tales on just how they got to us. One lady had a wall fall on top of her, crushing her spine. She managed to scramble free using her arms and then was carried by a passer-by to a local clinic that had also been raised to the ground. Then she was carried to a field hospital in Port Au Prince, then boarded a US medical ship, then to a tent in the Catholic hospital by helicopter, and now to us. Her first x-rays of her spine (like all of our patients) were done two to three weeks after the injury.

I will write a longer, more detailed post for the medics amongst you soon but these patients have an assortment of T10 to L5 vertebral fracture-dislocations that are so obvious I soon had taught our following journalist to interpret them with confidence and to start predicting the neurological deficit. Not surprisingly, neurologically, almost all have complete spinal cord injuries. The medical and nursing care they are receiving here is very basic but very good given the circumstances.

I duly completed the first ever medical ward round in Haiti's brand new spinal hospital, and fielded the same question repeatedly from every patient.

''Will I walk again?' they asked and with as much honesty as I could muster, I answered with a message to stay positive and have hope, followed by an awkward, and I rather suspect, an unconvincing smile.

Shammy, before I forget, just to let you know, the tympanic thermometer you donated was met with much happiness by the Haitian nurses when shown how to use it followed by laughter and clapping when it beeped and read a temperature. Thank you for that.

It has been a really emotional day although my writing I fear has been far too indifferent to express it truly. I am also scared I may not remember so many of the stories that ought to be heard. As I return to my sleep, my mind once again turns to one of our patients, that in the blink of an earthquake lost her husband, her child, five siblings, her parents and now left paraplegic and homeless. So I ask you all to look up to the skies on Valentines night, whomever your sharing it with, and spare a thought for those in this country and in our hospital (now lovingly named simply as 'The Unit'), struggling to cope with a new life under those same starry skies that shine down upon us all.

With love always,
Saqib

16.02.2010 – The Friendship Boots

Dear Readers,

Tonight I will write two days' worth of events. I could not write yesterday because electricity has been very intermittent here and I was unable to charge my phone. Although in all honesty, I was out like a Haitian light with no electricity myself and slept straight through my cockerel alarm clock. I shall write the stories of the past two days as separate letters because the contrast between the past two days has not been greater.

I start with a beautiful story (in my humble opinion) and it is definitely the story I had hoped to find for you all before Valentine's Day. I apologise for the late arrival!

On Valentine's Day itself I was feeling rather forlorn. Perhaps it was the heat, the long journey, being tired, the basic food sustaining me, thoughts of loved ones at home or perhaps it was a combination of these.

However, at work, the physiotherapist and I decided to make some splints for the patients' feet as they were all developing contractures of their ankles (because they cannot move them). We did not have any material to do so but instead went around all the patients deciding on who would need them and we could prioritise whatever supplies we did have.

In one of our 'wards' of the 'spinal unit' we have three female patients, all paraplegic, all in their twenties (including the one who has lost every member of her family). Remarkably, these three patients have travelled their entire journey together since the earthquake. They met in a field hospital in Port Au Prince, went onto the USS Comfort (the US medical ship) together, were then offloaded at the tented hospital and then transported to ours. The three of them have become close friends whilst having to spend the last month together immobile, each with their variety of pressure sores. Indeed, the three friends refused to be transported to our unit unless they all came together.

Between them they are a very happy group and always greet any entrant into their ward with a loud 'BOUNJOUR!' and a giggle or a bout of singing. However, on this Valentine's Day they were rather quiet as I entered with the physio, especially the woman who lost everyone, a tear in her eyes as she stared vacantly at the wall.

Via the interpreter, another of the three women asked me why it was that some patients with similar problems had operations and she did not. I truly was stumped and said something like 'for the back injuries we don't have any reliable operations' before tailing off unconvincingly.

She then said in the other hospital they sat her up out of bed. I replied that we will soon get her a strong brace for her back and with the physiotherapy, start to sit her up and give her lots of exercises. She looked and then smiled the broadest, warmest, excited smile I have ever seen that melted me to a complete pulp.

In the meantime, the physio had somehow looked under her bed and found a wonderful pair of brand new, purpose made ankle splints (in a very funky shade of bright blue). The patient then told us she received them at a previous hospital but had since stopped using them. We could not believe our luck as now we too were all smiling at each other.

However having one proper set of splints did not solve the problem of the other patients and it would be wrong for the one patient in the ward to have the only pair. So we came up with a simpler idea. We asked the owner of the boots whether she was happy to share with the other two friends. She said yes and I told her the boots would be a sign of their friendship for each other. We then devised a two hourly rotation policy so they would swap over the boots regularly. We wrote the rotation programme on their wall with the title 'friendship boots' in bold colours which had them all giggling again.

But it was in the evening that Valentine's Day truly became magical. The founder of the charity and his wife bought decorations, balloons, sweets and a large chocolate cake with the word 'love' on it. Then all the volunteers from the UK walked back to the hospital in the evening when the patients were not expecting us. And suddenly we were singing 'Happy Valentine's Day to everyone' in the tune of 'Happy Birthday'. It was quite surreal but we could not think of anything more original to sing. The cake and sweets were then distributed to patients as well as putting heart shaped stickers on their gowns.

All the patients and relatives were laughing and smiling and there was an epic joy and vibrancy in the ward that I could not explain as everyone hugged and took photos. I remained stunned by the love and generosity of the people running this charity and during that evening, for the first time in my life, I wished I was nowhere else in the world but right there at that very moment witnessing such an amazing Valentine's Day created by such extraordinary people.

I truly hope you all had as special Valentine's Day as I.

In other news, the American medics are in town and we have our first quadriplegic patient (cannot move arms or legs) on the unit and the children's home we are staying in is now busy with children with disability (they come on the weekdays), including one eight-month-old child abandoned because she had hydrocephalus (swollen head because of too much water on the brain). She was found and cared for by the same young British couple building this hospital.

Soon I will write today's story titled 'The school has collapsed'...

With happy and now sad love,
Saqib

16.02.2010 – The School Has Collapsed

Dear Readers,

Let me now slowly start to introduce the characters of this story. Firstly, and most importantly, there is Carwyn and Reninca. Carwyn is one of the two actors who initially set up this project and Reninca is his wife. Carwyn and Reninca have been living here permanently for the last year trying to set up this project. They are both still in their twenties and are the couple that are looking after us (and everyone and everything else it seems!).

Today, at midday, Carwyn came inside to the 'spinal unit' (he is normally outside organising and overseeing the surrounding confusion of building sites). He told us a school in the town had collapsed and further details were unknown. He was taking the ambulance and needed medical personnel urgently.

A nurse (whom I will introduce soon) and I hurriedly packed what flimsy equipment we had and soon jumped in the back of the ambulance. With us was another volunteer from the UK, an interpreter and our lab technician. As we sped with the ambulance lights and siren blazing through the rickety potholed streets of Cap-Haitien amongst the static yet bustling traffic, I wondered to myself why we needed a lab technician. It was only when she answered her phone, started screaming and wailing that I understood why she was with us and had more of an idea of what kind of catastrophe we were speeding to.

Once we arrived, jumping out of the back of the ambulance into more rain filled potholes, we made our way through swarms of crowds gathered at the site. We battled our way through frantic and distressed onlookers, dressed in our surgical scrubs, stethoscopes on our necks and a hotchpotch of medical aid on our backs. We finally all scrambled into the school premises that were manned by guards preventing the crowds bursting in.

The front of the school building itself was intact but the back portion had collapsed. A landslide from an adjacent hill had crushed the supporting walls, the second floor more severely affected than the first.

As we entered the school premises, I noticed the following people: approximately fifteen UN soldiers, the same number of US soldiers, a scattering of Haitian police, the Canadian police, many Haitian men with no obvious affiliation and more journalists and random people taking photos than the rest of the others put together. I looked around and noticed that myself and the nurse were the only medics on the scene.

Some of the UN and US personnel were working indoors with the Haitians, preventing anyone from entering, explaining the building needed to be stabilized. They had already identified one child's body with an unknown number of others inside.

The next hour was as disorganised and unstructured as the very Haitian buildings that are built in the town. It seems each house is built like an upside-down pyramid, one small ground floor, followed by a second floor that is even bigger than the ground floor and a third floor on top of that which extends beyond the second floor.

Whilst waiting, we decided to at least prepare what little we had. Back in the UK I have recently started a routine of inventing a new surgical instrument or tool for every operation I am involved in. I normally think of an invention mid-operation and proudly announce it to my groaning boss as he replies, "What is it now?" Most of the time I am pleasantly surprised when I am told it has already been invented or told to stop being so ridiculous. However, on this stark occasion outside a collapsed school in Haiti, I was not inventing equipment. I was wishing for the most basic kit imaginable - a guedel airway, a bag and mask, a cannula larger then 22G, portable oxygen. We simply did not have any of it.

Eventually we were permitted to set up our stretcher area in the downstairs of the school that had now been deemed safe. And soon the men working upstairs could be heard moving rubble before a sudden flurry of activity as the first child was bought down.

We placed a young boy, no more than eight years old, onto the stretcher and examined him amongst the commotion. We frantically looked for any signs of life, following any systematic protocol we have been taught as medical professionals. But we soon realised this poor child had lost his life under the rubble, and we placed the boy into a body bag that had clearly been bought by someone knowing to expect the worst.

And the next child was rushed down from the carnage, a young girl. Dead.

And the next child, dead.

And the next child, dead

The story, I was told later, is that these four children would always sit together every day and play together, refusing to sit apart. It was with great tragedy that this friendship too resulted in them dying together. As I placed the last child into the body bag, I noticed a man who had fought his way through the crowd and look at this child in particular. And then I saw him stumble and stutter backwards and silently start crying in the corner of the room. And no one was near him. I quickly took my leave from the body bag and walked up to his corner and put my arm around him, the father of the child. I could not say anything and nor could he as he quietly wept.

One of the children who died today was the only child of the medical director of the charity I am volunteering with, a doctor who has spent a year dedicated to setting up the project. It truly makes you wonder about the absurdity of fate. In a country that has already been hit with an earthquake, there is a landslide. The landslide only affected one building. The building was a primary school. At the time of the landslide, the school was occupied with studying children. Although tragic that four children died, one was the only child of the one doctor who has been trying to make this whole place better.

One of the most vivid memories I will take with me throughout my life is the satchel of one of the children, discarded on a dusty floor, with a colourful book poking out, "My book of science".

With love always,
Saqib

18.02.2010 - The US Marines Fly In And Bring Vital Aid

Dear Readers,

At midday there was a ruckus outside our unit and a large crowd had suddenly gathered. I looked out and saw everyone in the crowd looking to the sky. And then I heard a loud, chopping, whirring noise rumbling in the air. I too looked up and saw a dark green helicopter with a colourful blue and orange tail, circling our hospital grounds over and over again like an eagle scouring for its prey. It circled at least fifteen times before it began its descent, swooping down onto a landing area on a field that the eagle had clearly deemed safe. As the propellers neared the earth, they sent out a noise and gust of wind so powerful it blew every loose piece of debris from the ground flying upwards and into the crowd. We all turned our backs and covered our ears as twigs and small stones came flying towards us.

The helicopter landed and when the propellers simmered to a gentle halt, five people climbed out of the already open doors. Imagine your perfect scene from a cheesy army movie. In classic movie style, almost in slow motion, out came four very tall, well-built American navy soldiers, dressed in full combat gear. Next to them was a smaller, older lady, in civilian clothes. The five of them walked in a perfect horizontal line. In the middle was the eldest of the soldiers and presumed leader with a commanding, short buzzed grey hair. Next to him on his left was a soldier with a Polish name I could not pronounce. And to the commander's right were two of the younger soldiers, wearing shades, one Haitian American and one Hispanic named Gomez to complete the total cliché of movie stars. The woman of course was the logistical support for an NGO working with them.

One of the soldiers was carrying a small cardboard box, I was not sure why. I hoped it may be some vital supplies we had requested. As the group got closer and closer, I peeked at the box to see what the US navy had bought us...... A box of pop tarts! I kid you not. It was such an extraordinary and hilarious image! I have never been so delighted! This was definitely a movie I would pay to watch!

The US soldiers were actually from the USS Comfort, the renowned American medical ship. It was apparently docked near Haiti at the time of the earthquake. The leader of the soldiers (the older one in the middle with the grey hair) was actually a trauma surgeon who explained their mission. They were scouring Haiti for any remainder of earthquake victims that still needed specialist care. The mandate was specific. Any operation that could be completed in Haiti should be done in Haiti, any patients requiring more complex care were allowed to be taken back to the ship.

The trauma surgeon went on to tell me the work carried out by them in the immediate aftermath on the quake. Twelve operating theatres, all utilized constantly, twenty-four hours a day for an entire month. He said over 95% of the estimated trauma surgery for the victims had now been completed with just a few new cases being identified. We showed them around the spinal unit and highlighted some of the patients that we thought would benefit from spinal surgery.

Unfortunately, only one patient possibly met their criteria - one of the three close friends I mentioned earlier in a post 'The Friendship Boots'. I scratched my head and considered the ethical and social implications for the three of them if one is whisked away for an operation whilst the other two remained. They will likely be each other's support network for a long time and to create a clear division may be catastrophic for this bond. It would be an operation none of them would ever understand. As of yet, no clear decision has been made by the US surgical team.

In the meantime, I have cheekily self-appointed myself as the medical director of the spinal unit and will start writing up medical management plans for everything from catheter management, thromboprophylaxis, drugs formularies, antibiotic guidelines to social and psychological care, specifically tailored to the total lack of facilities here - all whilst chewing on a cinnamon pop tart. With love,
Saqib

19.02.2010 – One Step Closer To The Epicentre

Dear Readers,

Today I write with a shake back to earthquake reality. Up until now I have described only the beginning foundations of our spinal unit with our handful of spinal patients. Essentially, I have described a specialist tertiary referral centre being built for a specific type of injury pattern.

Although it is really exciting to be present at the beginning of a wonderful project and be able to offer much needed medical input, I have been acutely aware that this was the tip of a very large iceberg that's balancing precariously on another massive iceberg that's melting very slowly in the rather disappointing Haitian weather (raining most days).

Today our team visited the Catholic hospital along with its additional tented wards, ten kilometres away but still a 45 minute drive as the pothole between the two hospitals has only a little half built road on it. We visited to gather much needed supplies, identify more patients that are suitable for transfer to our unit and generally observe. This particular hospital has had a long history and support of an American charity for many years and since the earthquake, a very experienced and passionate surgeon has converted it into a hospital ready to receive the injured from Port Au Prince. Other government hospitals, I am told, have been less keen to accept foreign intervention, at least on such a scale. The hospital has been taking all sorts of patients, predominantly with orthopaedic injuries and I would classify it as a secondary referral centre, the primary centres of course being the field and makeshift hospitals in Port Au Prince. However, like all other hospitals throughout the country, it is totally overwhelmed.

The established inpatient wards are full and the Americans have erected seven field tents on the hospital grounds, each bursting with patients. I took a tour with an internal medicine physician whom I met on the bus journey into the country and we were both happy to see each other again.

Each tent holds about fifty patients, lined up in two rows, twenty-five on each side. The patients lie in fold away beds that look more like large stretchers than hospital beds. The gaps between each stretcher are two feet at most. On the stretchers are the patients. In the gaps are the patients' relatives (often multiple per patient).

As I walked through, the scale of this disaster became just slightly more apparent. The first patient I saw was a teenager with bilateral above knee amputations, followed by more patients with various amputations of various limbs, multiple patients in plaster casts or external fixations and a whole new selection of more paraplegic patients to be admitted to our unit.

The atmosphere was chaotic at best but there was still a vibrant uplifting response from the patients and a palpable work ethic from the volunteers. The orthopaedic team was overwhelmed in theatres constantly debriding wounds and revising fixations whilst the tents were dutifully manned by an assortment of other specialist medical teams. I found it quite surreal as I soon found myself explaining some of the x-ray findings and management plans to a gynaecologist looking after all these patients in her tent.

I was shown another paraplegic patient, a sweet teenage girl, who lost both her parents in the quake. Her older brother was by her side and had not left her side for one moment since the disaster, day or night, holding her hand for as long as he could. "Yes", I said, "She should be transferred to the spinal rehab centre". She smiled.

I then visited the even more chaotic operating theatre complex and met the surgeon in charge.

'We need you', he said in a joyful American way.

'Yes Sir, I want to help with the operating or any other way', I said.

'Come tomorrow, eight AM sharp, you'll be operating all day, welcome to the team', as he patted me on the shoulder.

'No, Sir, I cannot come tomorrow', I said sadly as the kind surgeon looked at me oddly. So I continued my explanation.

'You see, tomorrow morning is the funeral of a child whom we pulled out of the rubble when a school collapsed. Her father is a doctor I know. I'd like to attend the funeral.'

'Oh' said the surgeon. 'Well our team leaves on Saturday. Perhaps next week you can help the new team'.

'Yes' I said, 'I will try'.

(Long conversation shortened)

In other news, I have started my Haiti Spinal Unit manual, outlining a ridiculously ambitious plan from medical and nursing care to housing and employment opportunities in the long term for the patients. One of my patients has become very sick. And in the evening I sat and bottle fed the cutest baby with disabling hydrocephalus, in quiet contemplation, that even being one step closer to the epicentre, I cannot comprehend the scale of the disaster.

"300,000 injured", they say. "40,000 amputations", they say.

Today I have seen the absolute mania required to care for just over 400 of those victims.

"Holy smokes", I say.

With love always,
Saqib

20.02.2010 – A Funeral In Haiti And A Prayer For You All

Dear Readers,

I write in a sad and sombre mood. I start with a verse from the Bible I read whilst at church today and dedicate it to the people of Haiti.

'So I returned, and considered all the oppressions that are done under the sun: and behold the tears of those oppressed, and they had no comforter; and on the side of their oppressors there was power. I praised the dead which are already dead more than the living which are yet alive. Better is he than both they, which has not yet been born, who has not seen the suffering that occurs under the sun.' -Ecclesiastes Chapter 4 Verses 1-3

I never thought I would come to Haiti and attend a funeral. Today I did. The chain of events that led to this day has been very unfortunate. For those who have not followed my previous letters, I shall quickly recap. On Monday, in a country devastated by a recent earthquake, there was a landslide. The landslide affected only one building in the town, a primary school. The primary school had children studying inside. A nurse and I were the only medics on the scene of total mayhem. Four children were pulled out. All four were dead, confirmed by myself and the nurse and placed into body bags. Of the four children, out of the seventy five attending, one was the only child of the Haitian medical director driving the charity to build our hospital.

As the team began getting ready for the service, it dawned on me I had never been to a Christian funeral let alone a Haitian one. I certainly did not have the appropriate smart black clothes, my entire wardrobe consisting of cargo pants, T-shirts, hospital scrubs and mud filled trainers. However, the hospital administrator (the smartest dressed man in the hospital and perhaps Haiti itself) kindly invited me to his house to lend me a suit. Remarkably, despite being 2 inches taller than me, his suit and shoes were a rather good fit.

The hospital staff and the British volunteers then travelled in typical 4th world* (see end note) style to the church, twenty-three smartly dressed adults crammed into a minibus with a capacity of twelve and a windscreen with more cracks than clear glass.

The church itself was not grand but large and eloquent, brimming full of six-hundred mourners to pay their respects to the doctor's child. Soothing organ music was played as a queue had formed to greet the grieving family at the front. As I got to the front, I saw the coffin with a wreath of flowers, the words 'profond regret l'ecole primarie' and a photograph of a sweet eight year old girl. I flashbacked to the day of the incident, the girl I saw was more debris and dust than skin.

It was only when I saw a row of other children from the same school walk past with tears in their eyes that my eyes too started to well. And when I gave my condolences to each member of the family, some of the women wailing loudly, the child's father took my hand and whispered simply 'thank you doctor'.

The service continued in Creole and French with intermittent breaks of beautiful hymns from a choir in formation behind the pulpit. I gather during the service the British medical team was thanked for their presence on the emergency scene but there was only one part of the service I understood.
The child's father had said a few words to the mourners, standing strongly at the pulpit before the very end, he said, 'au revoir ma fille, au revoir ma fille, au revoir ma fille' and burst into tears. At some stage during the service, each one of us shed more than just one tear.

The coffin and congregation then transferred to the cemetery, a scenic location outside of the city, with the overlooking mountains in the background and lush gardens in the foreground.

As a violin began to play and the coffin began to be lowered under the earth, there was another volley of uncontrollable wailing as women flung themselves to the ground as others frantically consoled them whilst more of our team members began to silently weep.

My mind began drifting to the sad moments associated with my own life and then I began thinking of the estimated one-hundred-thousand people buried in mass graves outside of Port Au Prince just one month ago, unidentified, undignified. No goodbyes. No beautiful funeral. No ceremony. No prayers.

And I lowered my head in prayer to the God of the Haitian people, and to the God of all people worldwide, and to the God of the major world religions, and to the God of all the other religions. And to the God of the religions that have no God. I prayed He would give the Haitian people strength in their time of loss. And I prayed He would give all the people in the world strength in their moments of need, because in our saddest and darkest moments, no matter our race, religion or language, it is still the same colourless and transparent tears within us all that flow from our hearts and out through our eyes.

With love, sadness and profound regret,
Saqib

*my definition of 4th World - 3rd World country + crippling natural disaster

25.02.2010 – Voodoo and Surgical Bad Spirits

Dear Readers,

Voodoo is a religious fusion between ancient West African rituals and Catholicism. The slave masters enforced their Christian beliefs onto the slaves whilst the slaves hid their ancient religious practices underground or under Catholic terminology. Over time, the two have become rather intertwined, unable to separate one from the other, almost like an unhappy couple, a forced marriage.

The Voodoo God is Bonjwe (French: bon dieux: good god). Bonjwe is the creator of the world but has no direct involvement in the running of day to day life. Instead there are Iwa, or spirits, which can be prayed to and called upon. These spirits have their own stories, cool and hot spirits, bad and good ones. Amidst the hybrid-catholic (con)fusion, these spirits were named as Christian saints.

In Haiti, voodoo culture is very popular. Unfortunately, I have not had much exposure to it, often being told it's a terrible thing by our Baptist hosts. They say there are many dark rituals performed including sacrifice and zombitication, bringing the dead back to life. However, these ancient practices are shrouded in mystery and not accessible to the outside world. The only exposure I have heard is at night, when one can often hear the rhythmic beat of voodoo drums in the distance.

Medically, inexplicable diseases or illness are often attributed to bad spirits or curses. For example, an epileptic seizure is a bad spirit or a disabled child has been cursed. I have often seen this mentality in other parts of the world and merely put it down to poor education and misunderstanding.

Our ambulance recently got called out for a medical emergency. A doctor was also requested to go to the scene so

I grabbed my newly created emergency kitbag (lessons learnt from the school collapse) and jumped into the ambulance.

An hour and a half later we were still on the road, or rather a dirt track, bumping our way through the Haitian mountains. At one stage we passed through a plateau with an almost 360 degree view of stunning hills and mountains around us. I was tempted to ask the driver to let me out so I could enjoy the scenery and he could pick me up on the way back.

Once we drove through more streams and small rivers, we arrived at a scene of commotion. I jumped out fearing another disaster but instead witnessed a young man sitting on the rocks, ranting and raving to himself. He was surrounded by a gathering of onlookers.

From a medical point of view, it was obvious there was no acute physical emergency. But the patient had a feared glazed look in his eyes as he aggressively clapped the shoes he was holding together and repeated the same words over and over in Creole 'the blood of Christ, the blood of Christ, the blood of Christ'. He would not let anyone near him, attacking anyone who got close, sometimes whispering the same phrase, sometimes screaming it.

Taking a very basic history from the locals, I gather the patient had no previous problems and had not said anything for a day before starting this crazed rant. A pastor at the scene asked me what my thoughts were. I was tempted to say 'delirium' or 'acute psychosis' but realised he would not understand my English nor the terminology. He looked again at me with expectant eyes and I scratched my head.

'Bad spirit?' he asked.

'Yes, bad spirit', I agreed as we bundled the patient into the ambulance along with 20 odd relatives and spent the long scenic journey home listening to the screams of the 'blood of Christ' coming from the back.

The next day I returned to the Catholic hospital, helping with wounds and basic orthopaedic procedures, removing and resetting plaster casts, manipulations of bones. It was here I realised how much the experience in South Africa had given me. After a while I peeked into the operating room to see what was going on. The US orthopaedic surgeons were fixing a patient's femur. Three surgeons were scrubbed in, the main surgeon being rather upset with how the procedure was progressing.

I was soon assisting with positioning the x-ray machine. The operation itself should not have taken more than one hour but three and a half hours later they were still at it, struggling to come to terms with the unfamiliar kit. Anything that could have gone wrong did go wrong with the lead surgeon muttering under his breath trying to figure out what the problems were. Two of the surgeons simultaneously gave themselves needle stick injuries and towards the end of the operation when the old surgeon banged his head of the theatre lights, I could not help but laugh as I wondered too if he had bad spirits.

In slightly more positive terms, I now have the US Comfort Navy medical ships phone number on my contact list and have been in email communication with their personnel. I have successfully referred one of our spinal patients to be picked up by helicopter, taken to the ship and be operated on which I feel is quite a unique achievement, to successfully refer a patient back to the US military. I even have a personal email from the US military apologising for their slow and disorganised response because their server was not working properly. Quite a unique yet worrying souvenir in my opinion!

With love,
Saqib

25.02.2010 – Heroes And Goodbyes

Dear Readers,

Wherever we travel in our lives, no matter for how long or short, we always leave our footprint and a small piece of ourselves. Tonight, I write my final footprint and my last letter, under the same star-studded sky that greeted me on my arrival.

I would be lying if I said I had specifically fallen in love with the Haitian people. Like all peoples, there are both the beautiful and the unsavoury characters amongst them. And like all impoverished people throughout the world, they are dignified, hard-working, humble and gracious. But throughout my journey here, I have fallen in love with a specific number of wonderful people I have met along the way.

These last two weeks, there was always a recurring thought in my mind at night as I drifted to sleep.

'What would I do if there was an earthquake right now?'

And my answer would always be turn my back to the collapsing roof and cover my head. My injuries would almost certainly be to my spine, crushed under the weight of the falling rubble. I think of the devastating injuries and paralysis I may suffer and then I shake my head thinking it could never happen. And then I remember the patients on my ward, the maths teacher, the construction worker, the student nurse, the pastor's wife, the mother of three small children and other patients who probably all did the same as I would in an earthquake, turn their back, and become paralysed. And suddenly there is a face to my imagined injury and the whole scenario becomes all too real.

But these faces I know are smiling, happy and hopeful. In this story of the earthquake, these patients are the real heroes. Their resilience and determination is a testament to the strength of the human spirit within us all. Their ability to continue to laugh and smile is an indication there is a future still worth fighting for.

And then there are their family members who care for them. They wash, feed and clothe not just their own family, but also lovingly assist those patients that no longer have a family, day and night. Their stories are equally sad but their compassion for their loved ones and fellow sufferers is a wonderful display of unity in hard times.

And the many volunteers I met, those that had been here before the earthquake and those that came after, dropping whatever was going on in their own lives to assist those in desperate need, travelling vast distances to do so, showed that in times of disaster, natural or man-made, or indeed in any circumstance, the power of human love can overcome any obstacle, any barrier and any problem. The volunteers throughout this country show that with love, teamwork and a will to succeed, anything is possible no matter how impossible it truly seems. I hope this is the final message of this story.

On the bus journey out of the country, I met another volunteer, a very nice Hispanic looking man from Texas in his fifties. We shared our stories and I told him of the cold showers each morning, the basic and limited food, the lack of electricity, the uncomfortable bedding and the muddy clothes. As we crossed the border, he pointed backwards and said,

'Back there, we were living in the moment'.

I was not quite sure what he meant but I found myself agreeing. I am mostly a quiet man. I rarely share my rambling writings and thoughts with anyone but myself. Somehow this time, I felt the story of the Haitian people needed to be told to all who would willingly read and I have vulnerably exposed my thoughts to you all. I wrote all my posts on my very basic phone in the late of night, each post like a gigantic text message that will surely make my mobile phone company very happy with my bill. I hope it will be a price worth paying for such a story.

So for all those that have allowed me to share my journey with you and the many of you that replied with messages of support, I thank you, your emails were my candles in the Haitian darkness. For all those that silently read along, I will never know if you were there or not, but if you have got this far and are still somehow reading, I thank you for being there, you were my matches ready to be sparked into light. And finally, for all those whose inboxes I spammed and my letters were unwelcome, I apologise wholeheartedly, I was your Haitian darkness.

I have said my goodbyes to my patients, not knowing if I will ever see these people again and also fearing the bleak future that awaits them all. I softly said the only three words that seemed appropriate at the time, to each one of them as I shook their hand or kissed their cheek in an embrace, the same three words I leave you all within a similar embrace and shake of the hand.

'God bless you'

With love
Saqib

Pakistan (2010)

In late July 2010, heavy monsoon rains flooded the Indus river basin in Pakistan, resulting in one-fifth of the country's total land area seriously affected by an unprecedented flood. Data suggests twenty million people were affected by the floods, destroying property, livestock and local infrastructure. The death toll was estimated at approximately two-thousand lives. At the time, the UN Secretary-General described it as the worst disaster he had ever seen, and concerns were raised that aid was not arriving fast enough to the affected populations.

I had recently finished my role as tutor for the MSc in Trauma Surgery at Swansea University, and in August 2010, was due to start as a trauma and orthopaedic registrar at the Birmingham Children's Hospital. After a few years away from the Midlands, it was exciting to be returning home once more. After the experience in Haiti, I had also enrolled in the Diploma of Catastrophe Medicine (DMCC) to further educate myself about healthcare in disaster zones.

I had heard briefly about the calamity of the floods starting in Pakistan. However, I had recently personally boycotted following any news stories from my country of origin, for all the reports of war, terrorism, natural and man-made disasters filled me with great sadness.

However, on my first day at my new post at the Birmingham Children's Hospital, I was informed that some relevant paperwork had not yet been processed and I was unable to start until it was cleared. Somewhat taken aback, I asked how long the delay might be but no one was able to give a clear response. At the same time, a friend mentioned that a healthcare organisation by the name of Doctors Worldwide, based in Manchester, UK, were urgently looking for a medical professional to perform an urgent needs assessment in an area of Pakistan severely affected by the floods – an area of Pakistan they were previously established in.

And so with the permission of my family, and some rather urgent, haphazard planning, I found myself boarding an aeroplane to Islamabad, Pakistan, the very next day.

05.08.2010 – From The City Of My Birth To The Land Of My Forefathers

Dear Family, Friends, Readers,

I am writing from Birmingham airport. I will soon be journeying to Pakistan with an international organisation assisting in the current humanitarian crisis after the unprecedented floods.

Yesterday morning, I truly was as giddy as a schoolboy starting a new job. It felt as though I was wearing a new school uniform, carrying my trusted satchel and jumping into my father's car as he drove me to the train station for my first day at school. As a child, I used to wait on this station's platform for seven years, usually tired and usually late, ready for the train to kidnap me away to a school far away from home. However, on this morning, my first day at school was at the Birmingham Children's Hospital, working as a paediatric orthopaedic registrar. I felt at peace, as though I was finally returning home, working in Birmingham, the beloved city of my birth and ready for the challenges ahead.

I was fortunate enough to be working with an old and trusted friend of mine and happily greeted him in the hospital foyer. We discussed our respective fortunes, misfortunes and future aspirations. I described some of my recent experiences and my current excitement towards this new post in Birmingham.

However, by midday of the induction programme, I was informed that some of my routine application forms had not been processed and it could take up to four weeks for me to be able to start my post. I shrugged and smiled, knowing I could at least use this time to complete some of my rather less glamorous research projects.

At the very moment that I was informed of this delay, my friend remembered an e-mail he had received that very morning, requesting immediate medical assistance in the developing catastrophe of extreme flooding in Pakistan. They requested for medical personnel who could travel within 48 hours. I scratched my head with great uncertainty and scoured my heart before making the relevant phone calls.

Pakistan is a country that has always scared me. It is a poor nation and through the lens of the media, it is a country plagued by the destruction of constant turmoil, gruesome internal conflict and political instability. It truly is a tragic nation. From the recent earthquake, to the very recent plane crash to the latest disaster of the floods, the people of Pakistan seem to be besieged with ongoing suffering. It was ironically just over 48 hours ago that I had consciously decided not to follow any more news reports from Pakistan, such was the constant tragedy that poured from the country.

And yet it is the country that holds the final resting place of my grandparents, inspiring humans that I have both met and never met. It was only this year that I discovered the diaries of my maternal grandparents, discovering how they fought through individual struggle and battled for a better future in the land that is now wrought with so much misery. Reading their words from as early as the 1930's, made me realise that for all its crippling flaws, the country of Pakistan is still safeguarding my past. So, just as I was returning as a giddy schoolboy to Birmingham yesterday morning, today I unexpectedly sit at the airport ready to return as a grown-up man to the land of my forefathers.

I am travelling with Doctors Worldwide, an organisation in the country which is already operational on the ground for the assistance of flood victims. I plan to travel for two weeks, although I realise two weeks are merely a moment in the lifetime of those suffering in Pakistan. For what I may be able to contribute, if anything at all, I know it will be fleeting. But I hope you do not think me an attention seeking maverick (or perhaps I am), for since my return from Haiti I have tried to stay involved with the Haiti Hospital Appeal project there as much I can. I hope I have been useful to them with what little knowledge I have and I am sure the Welsh surgical team that followed my journey found my descriptions to be accurate and helpful.

I know it may seem this random letter is unsurprising from me but sometimes I genuinely am surprised how I have lurched and fallen from one ridiculous scenario to another over these short years. I hope to document my experience in Pakistan in a similar fashion to that of Haiti if it is possible, for no other reason than it allows me to clear the thoughts that whir and whirl within my head. For those readers, allowing me to do this, I cannot thank you enough for reading and encouraging me.

I am aware of the hazards and dangers involved but I am sure all will be well, with the grace of God. I will leave with the same statement I wrote before I left for Haiti, that should I ever lose touch or contact, it is the ones I love the most who will be the last thought on my mind before I close my eyes to sleep at night. For those that know me best, you know who you are.

With love,
Saqib

06.08.2010 – The God Of Water

Dear Readers,

I have arrived safely in Pakistan with very little sleep on the flight. I decided to move straight up to the affected area with the local representative of the organisation I am with after completing some formalities in Islamabad. I am currently staying comfortably in a guesthouse near Noshera, a city in shock. I am now awakened and refreshed by an unavoidable cold shower!

I have always been fascinated by water, its formations and its freedoms. For me, there is always a wonderful feature about it, a majestic, hypnotic, God like quality. The endless horizon of the Indian Ocean that I admired from a deserted South African beach represented the infinite, the endless, the known and the unknown, for I could never know what was on the other side of the horizon. The bobbing waters of the Swansea marina were calm, tranquil and peaceful whereas the fountain displays outside the tallest building in the world were full of mesmerising grandeur and elegance. But today I witnessed the ugly, demonic side of water and my admiration of it has completely vanished. If it has God like qualities, then the floods in Pakistan were its power, its ferocity and its total and ruthless ability to destroy. As we drove through the remnants of a devastated city, the water had all but fled to its lower grounds, leaving behind just murky and dirty pools of brown water amongst drenched buildings, accompanied by a foul smell for an added measure of unnecessary punishment. My new colleague showed me photographs of the very city taken by himself three days ago, as people waded and battled through rising water levels just to survive.

We visited some of the existing camps within the city, the largest housing six hundred displaced and now homeless families with an estimated three-thousand-five-hundred people within the walls of the camp. Conditions were bleak, the basics of sanitation, clean water, food and healthcare all stretched to the limit. Tents clustered together with little space between them and within each tent was nothing but a mat and a person sitting on it, staring vacantly. There are spots of litter and stagnant water everywhere. However, there is general order and calm in the camp and as always within these horrific situations, there are those care-free children whom I could not resist myself to take a cheeky photo with.

Tomorrow we travel to the surrounding villages and areas where support has not yet arrived. We have acquired some equipment and medications as well as food aid. The descriptions from other organisations and local sources suggest there are many cases of skin infections, gastrointestinal infections and injuries. I have been humbled and blessed by the moral, emotional and physical support already offered to me by countless people in Pakistan whom I know only through family and friends. I cannot thank you enough.

With love always,
Saqib

07.08.2010 – The Waters Are Rising, The Road Is A River

Dear Readers,

Heavy rains did not wake me on my first night as I slept comfortably through a severe downpour. By the morning, the water levels had risen somewhat again, swamping the very area we had planned to visit and assess for our proposed clinic site.

As we waited for the weather conditions to improve, we hurriedly transferred all our equipment and medication stock into one central location, allowing us to systematically calculate which supplies we had in order to be an effective functional unit and determine which supplies we were still missing. My colleague and veteran of Doctors Worldwide projects in Pakistan then scoured through the local town collecting further vital supplies whilst I was joined by a retired army medical dispenser, whose home had been destroyed. Together we organised all our medications and documented them into a pharmacy inventory. This time I remembered to check for and note the expiry dates of the stock, a mistake I had previously made in Haiti.

By the afternoon, the rain had ceased and we decided to drive towards our proposed clinic site. Along the journey, there were makeshift tents dotted around the countryside as a man washed his clothes in a stagnant pool of mud and a baby was being washed in an adjacent pool of murky water. As we ventured further, the small puddles on the road started to unite into larger puddles and the larger puddles then pooled together into a shallow stream. Believing this was the worst of the conditions, we crept forward before the shallow stream that was previously a road became a deeper stream and at its worst, two to three feet deep. This road, forty-eight hours ago, was perfectly driveable.

As I rolled up my trousers and was prepared to jump out to

wade back, expecting our car to begin swimming rather than driving, miraculously we pushed forward through many streets and found higher ground again. The scenes either side of us were despotic as people carried their possessions back and forth through floating rubble, buildings and houses destroyed on either side of the road. Occasionally a truck managed to pass through, distributing food and water, but these people were clearly isolated from any significant aid.

We passed through a further village before arriving at the suggested makeshift clinic site at dusk. However, the fields were waterlogged, and although the river flowing in the vicinity was beautifully serene amidst the backdrop of rising hills, the location was not comforting for our purposes.

We made a quick decision to abandon this location as night was soon approaching and we still had the river road to cross. On the return journey, we passed many people that again were carrying their possessions out of the area. They had only just returned to reclaim their homes and dried their possessions when the water rose again. On the way back we picked up a family of five with three small children who were evacuating the area for the second time, making a three hour journey by foot with their meagre possessions on their backs and one's heart could not help but bleed for them.

We made it safely back as we re-evaluated our position. Our equipment and inventory are ready to be functional, it is just a matter of finding a place of need in such dire and unpredictable circumstances. Safety is of course paramount. Tomorrow morning, we get up early and drive to an abandoned district hospital to see whether it can be rejuvenated into life.

On a lighter note, for those who do not know me, I am proud to be co-founder of a comedy football team, the Dadyal Dice Rollers in Birmingham. Before I left for Pakistan, I had proudly designed a team-shirt with logo. The shirt image arrived by e-mail and I was so happy I placed it as my desktop wallpaper. My colleague noticed this badge and asked me what it was. After explaining, he said he too was a keen footballer and asked whether we should play football sometime. So, one of my new objectives is to organise a local football match with the kids, I always knew the Dadyal Dice Rollers would be an international team!

With love always,
Saqib.

09.08.2010 – Indiana Jones And The Raiders Of The Drowning Hospital

Dear Readers,

Seventy-two hours ago, whilst in Birmingham, before I had any idea I would be in Pakistan, I described to a friend an awesome medical career. I suggested a medical version of Indiana Jones where one would spend most of the time teaching at a University but then when the need for adventure arose, he would don his hat and leather jacket, travel to find the medical holy grail. I got duly laughed at!

This morning, after four hours' sleep, we ventured back towards the same flooded village we visited yesterday. After another rickety drive, we arrived behind the fields of an apparent abandoned healthcare facility. We trudged through vast amounts of mud and large puddles before passing a cemetery. Within the cemetery, many of the graves had crumbled and caved, crushing the inner walls, leaving it exposed to the open air. It was an eerie and disheartening vision. I asked permission to take a photograph and although it did not feel right to photograph, the images are so sad, I felt it worthwhile to document. I read a silent prayer for those hopefully still resting in peace.

We then made our way to the facility. Across the clinic's barbed wire, perched above ten foot walls, were debris from the floods, indicating the water had passed over the entire building. Inside the compound a few local people were sheltering amongst strewn litter and stagnant water.

We trespassed through to the back, where we discovered another building, a suitable size for a clinic. Again, mud and slime covered the walls like a monstrous painting. The doors were jammed, locked shut, stuck in inches of slime. My colleague climbed over the back gate in his bare feet and tried from the other side as we kicked the doors open, one after the other. And at that moment it felt crazy, kicking down the doors of a hospital and I wondered if Dr. Jones would be doing the same! Inside there was battered furniture and more slime then outside. I was told to look out for snakes and I started laughing before thinking, "Snakes, I hate snakes", in true Jones style. The compound has enormous potential. It needs serious work but we can get it functional very quickly. The cleaning process has already begun and the difference is phenomenal after a few hard-working volunteers contributed to the cause.

Having surveyed the region very quickly, it is apparent this medical clinic is the only one in the area and it serves a population (before the flood) of approximately 100,000 people. The demand is therefore likely to be huge. The facilities here are terrible. Our aim is to get the clinic functional, bring basic healthcare as soon as possible as well as start a food programme from within the quarters. Our self-imposed deadline is forty-eight hours, but I am hopeful we can achieve it within twenty-four hours.

I am aware of the high quality care our organisation wants to bring to the people of Pakistan and so it will be my duty to ensure we make this project start with rigorous standards. I know that once standards drop in this type of system, it is difficult to retrieve. Hygiene is my number one priority. However, there is another major concern, as the entire region once again is on high alert for further flooding and the hospital that has just begun being cleaned may again be affected as I type this very letter.

Further good news regarding the surging Dadyal Dice Rollers Football Club: I have identified a youth team programme in the area so we may start scouting for players to take over from our already ageing squad and I have also discovered a supply of Tiger biscuits. For those that do not know what Tiger biscuits are, they are magical biscuits that give Dadyali players super psychological strength. However, they were banned for being an unfair performance enhancing substance. Our scout said they were no longer available but clearly, they still are! I will sack the scout once I return to the UK.

With love always,
Indy.

10.08.2010 – Even Simple Village Medicine Is Complicated!

Dear Readers,

The current job at hand and workload is enormous and almost overwhelming. There is so much so do and such little time, effectively we are starting to run a primary healthcare facility from scratch, from the back of a hotel room. It is hard to know where to prioritise one's energy and yet have enough rest to maintain energy levels. It is for this reason I am going to cut my letter for today into numbered points. Writing these letters does offer some internal relief and structure to the jangling mind so I feel it necessary to plough on with my rambling.

1. We cracked open the other hospital building and found some wonderful goodies covered in slime: an upside-down doctor's desk, a drip stand, an examination table and most importantly, a dysfunctional light box (for viewing x-rays). I have always insisted that a functional clinic can only be considered functional if it has a dysfunctional light box. So, technically, we are fully established now!

2. The clean-up process of the buildings continues. Simply spraying the walls with water is not enough. We need to disinfect and repaint also as soon as possible.

3. The clinic has begun! Despite the work around us, patients have started to arrive and I started seeing patients. From complex orthopaedic trauma surgery in the NHS to backyard village medicine is quite a jump. However, local doctors are soon to be employed and hopefully I will learn from them as well as oversee the running of the clinic since I do not believe I am qualified to provide primary care consultations. The patients I am seeing so far are skin infections, multiple foot problems (I suppose that's what happens when you wade around in flood water for hours) and diarrhoea.

4. As stated earlier, hygiene is key. Too many times in Pakistan I have seen people throw litter. A staff worker drank his carton

of juice and promptly threw it into the wet fields. I explained this is unacceptable, firstly, it's not clean and secondly, some poor worker will have to now pick it up. It's time certain ideas need to be modernised. (Feel free to call me the dreaded infection control nurse!)

5. Each day on the drive to the hospital we drive past a cemetery. I learned from a recent diploma in catastrophe medicine that I completed that one could estimate the mortality rate based on new graves. And each day we drive past, there are new graves being made. I have no idea if this is the standard mortality rate here for the population or if it is flood related.

6. I still have so much administrating to do. I am calculating a cost analysis for the project, establishing clinical data collection and outcome measures, a rapid needs assessment of the population, inventory stock checks, accommodation for volunteers and of course, daily reporting to the organisation base in the UK.

7. I have finally had a warm shower as the weather is now improving. It is hot, hot, hot out here.

8. I have bought myself a South African rugby cap that I randomly saw in the local market. Having worked in South Africa for a year and watched Invicticus on the plane from Dubai, I thought it was ironic that they were selling a Bokke Rugby cap in cricket-mad Pakistan in the times of floods! I hope the Bokke will bring me luck! Anyhow, it will go nicely with my UN cap obtained from Haiti!

9. Help is on its way, I am in good health and well looked after! I am getting a few insect bites which is a slight concern given the amount of stagnant waters! I am aware the utmost priority is myself. Yesterday I was feeling dehydrated and lacking sleep so I came back to the hotel to load up on fluids and take a nap. I will take care of myself, I promise.

Work to do, apologies,
With love always,
Saqib

12.08.2010 – In Tribute And Admiration

Dear Readers,

As I drove the Doctors Worldwide Suzuki van at sunset on the M1 highway back up towards Noshera (after greeting our new volunteers and crucial team members at Islamabad airport the night before), I had the first opportunity to gather some thoughts that had been tinkering within my head and heart.

In Haiti, when I attended the collapse of a primary school and attended the subsequent funeral of one of the children, I wrote with such sadness that I know many readers cried at my emotional outpourings. In these letters, I have written optimistically and jovially about the positive aspects of the aid effort since I have realised in these extreme circumstances, words that make people cry only adds to the collective unhappiness in the world. But it has been a few days since I have learnt of the deaths of medical workers in Afghanistan, a location with a similar geopolitical climate to the one I am working in right now and it has plagued my mind. Some would say their work is rather worryingly similar to mine.

But rather than dwell on this, I wanted to pay tribute to these amazing people who tragically lost their lives whilst assisting with and improving the lives of others. I wanted to thank them, if only somehow I could, for the commitment and the ultimate sacrifice they made for a cause they believed in. But most of all I wanted to congratulate them, for being those human beings in this crazy world that realised that what they had been given in this life was enough for them to be happy, that they needed no more and would rather give away rather than accumulate, that they had found peace in finding a role to play in this world.

I will not write for others but I do often forget in the trivias and trials of my busy life, that the opportunities and possessions I have are also the unreachable aspirations of millions if not billions of less fortunate people in this world. When I remember this simple fact, I try to be thankful for what I have and not be too disheartened if, and often when, I cannot achieve more.

I have also wondered if I would have any regrets should the worst happen to me in this or any other situation. My only regret would be the pain I would cause deep in the heart of my parents for putting myself at risk. Yet it is the combined hearts of my father and mother that have led to the creation of this heart that writes these very words in this very situation. The end of my life is an inescapable fact, this cannot be changed. However, what can change is what can be achieved in the time I have been given. I would rather have a productive shorter life than a longer time in which I did not utilise the precious time I had for the objectives I want to achieve.

Although I was hoping to leave this story until the end of my journey, I want to share with you the story of my colleague with Doctors Worldwide whom has been working tirelessly with me on the ground. He has worked for the organisation for eight years in the region, including being involved in missions in Afghanistan in 2002 and Muzaffarabad after the earthquake in 2005. It was whilst working for Doctors Worldwide on different programmes he was unable to return home to say his farewells to both his dying mother and on a separate occasion, his dying three-year-old son. He speaks Urdu, English, Parsi, Pashto, Punjabi and is learning Turkish happily.

At the time of the floods in Noshera, he was once again working on a Doctors Worldwide programme to build a children's hospital in a different region, two hours' drive away. On that tragic day, he received a phone call from his family that the waters were rising nearby. He told them to monitor the situation closely. At nine a.m, he received a further phone call from his family that the waters are still rising. It was at this stage he realised something was drastically wrong and drove back as fast as he could. But due to the weather conditions and traffic, it took him five hours to return home. By that stage, the water in his house was waist deep. He quickly organised his family away from the area (including his one day old daughter) and proceeded to return to the house. He climbed over walls and rooftops to start retrieving possessions from his house and take them to higher ground on the third floor in hope that the water would not rise so high. This included his most prized possession, a twenty-year collection of books, his personal library. But the water kept rising and it was apparent he too needed to escape whilst his books drowned. He again climbed over sinking walls, running towards the car and fled with his family. All eight members of the family stayed in the car that night, in a tent the second night and the third day he took them to his family village for a place of safety in an unaffected area.

The next day he returned to the region and Doctors Worldwide mission began. He picked me up from the airport and the story you have read since are my letters. He has looked after me and watching him work is an inspiration, from his hard work to his resourceful ability to manage a project like this in such dire circumstances. He still has not had a chance to name his new baby daughter and has not seen her since the floods. "Afia", he says, as we drive up the motorway, "I have decided to name her Afia".

Dear readers, this is the true hero of this Pakistani tragedy and I enclose a photograph of him and myself, both standing on the roof of his house where the water level remains dangerously high. Jeremy, the hat he is wearing is one you wore on our three peaks challenge. I found it in the raincoat you gave to me before I left. I gave the hat to him. I hope you do not mind.

In further updates on our activity, the cooked food programme that Doctors Worldwide Is running has started remarkably well. It was wonderfully uplifting to see people returning home with their bowls of cooked rice and lentils. Ramadan has now started and to those celebrating, I wish you Ramadan Mubarak. To those who are not celebrating Ramadan, I also wish you Ramadan Mubarak!

With love always,
Saqib.

15.08.2010 – Meet The Doctors Worldwide Team

Dear Readers,

The last forty-eight hours have posed the greatest challenges and headaches to me since I arrived in Pakistan. I was not worried about suddenly dropping my plans in Birmingham and totally deviating off course to fly to Pakistan amidst the disaster. I was not worried by my lack of local language skills, I knew I would cope for my knowledge of basic Urdu was there. I was not worried about the well documented dangers in the country - I knew that if I was careful enough, I would stay out of trouble. I was not worried about flying out on my own with an organisation I knew very little about. I was not worried about not knowing who my team members would be in Pakistan when I arrived. I was not worried about having a very vague mandate and I was not worried about being assigned the team leader role to get the project off the ground.

The small team that we have, as you have seen from the work I have presented in these recent letters, is exceptionally efficient and organised. Our team originally started as just three in the whole of Pakistan (a medical student, the local Doctors Worldwide co-ordinator and myself) and within three days, we had cleaned out a destroyed healthcare centre, restocked it and began seeing patients. We were also regularly informing the media, both on Al-Jazeera and through various other websites of our activities. We were coordinating closely with our support team from the UK and most importantly, we were looking after each other and having fun with a great team spirit. Our e-mails were both filled with essential information but also jokes, poems, haikus and Shakespearean quotes. Our team became four with the arrival of another doctor from the UK who blended in beautifully to our work ethic and psyche. Our objectives became more defined, more streamlined and our machine was working very well. We gathered resources from local people and local volunteers who all have contributed an enormous amount.

My colleague and I were working almost 18-20 hours a day with many various aspects of the project to think about, working whilst eating lightly, working whilst driving and preparing for larger teams to arrive later with more specific skills. It was as almost as though we were a victim of our own success, for our reporting, communication, and field successes led to an influx of interest in our work. It was the sudden arrival or a Turkish team to join ours with very little warning which blew the well-oiled machine apart. We were not prepared at this stage for more volunteers, especially ones without language skills to communicate with. Being the team leader and suddenly being responsible for another four men (two doctors, two search and rescue staff) of which only one I could barely communicate with as the other three did not speak English or Urdu (only Turkish). Suddenly our lightning speed of movement has ground down to a gentle jog.

I believe my utmost priority is the safety of the staff under my care and it became apparent that this suddenly became an added burden and worry for I could not utilise them positively without worrying about their well-being. Our timings of work became delayed as we had to suddenly move out of our own hotel room to accommodate their presence and ensured their cooking requirements were met. The project suddenly became difficult to manage. However, this is the nature of disaster medicine and I have learnt a wonderful word from my Pakistani colleague, "juggar". It means to improvise and this is what we have done. I must ensure the project goes ahead as planned but also accommodate everyone in a useful way. For our new volunteers do not mean to be a hindrance and in fact our Turkish friends are a wonderful, noble and kind team. I am very happy they are here, just a little early unfortunately. However, they have great talents and skills too.

There are many definitions of leadership and one which I was taught recently at the Diploma in the Medical Care of Catastrophes was "a psychological ability to get others to complete specific tasks successfully". However, for me, the definition was not romantic enough. My definition is "having the ability to bring out the best in others whilst simultaneously bringing out the best in yourself". So the remainder of this post is dedicated to the best non-governmental organisation team in Pakistan in my biased opinion, the Doctors Worldwide team.

(These are the actual names we use in our e-mail banter to cheer each other up)

The Fantastic Mr Fox

Mr Fox is a post graduate 4th year medical student from Leeds University who happened to be on his medical elective in Islamabad during the time of the flood. He urgently looked around for others to help and found no assistance from local NGOs. Since he knew the Doctors Worldwide organisation in the UK, he appealed for help. It was he who got the project started. He has predominantly been working in Islamabad co-ordinating the mission from our headquarters there and also making trips up to the affected region.

In his spare emailing time he quotes Shakespeare, making me look rather uncultured. He has a wonderful sense of humour and tolerates my teasing of him very well. My only criticism of him is that he does not stroke his beard when he sits in a ponder!

The Pakistani 007

This man is the life and blood of the Pakistani Doctors Worldwide presence. He is a veteran of missions in Afghanistan and post-earthquake Pakistan. I have never quite met such a hardworking, passionate and truly resourceful man. His home was destroyed by the flood and it is him and I that have been working on setting up this flooded clinic. He is Bond because he drives his Suzuki car through rivers and climbs over walls like a secret agent.

Indiana Jones

This is me. This is because I wear silly hats, kick down doors and I hate snakes.

Cat woman

The Cat woman joined us five days into our mission and her role is also in Islamabad, coordinating with other NGOs, attending World Health Organisation meetings, organising volunteers and obtaining resources. She has a background in emergency medicine and is currently completing a full time Masters programme in Public Health Medicine. She is Cat woman because she says she is sassy but her claws and her teeth are sharp and feisty. She can certainly leap from meeting to meeting and still land on her feet.

Charlie

Charlie is one of the most experienced members of Doctors Worldwide and has been on previous medical expeditions to the Congo and Pakistan. He also has an emergency medicine background. He has been imparting his wisdom from the UK, ensuring our safety and giving important directions in our many different and difficult challenges. He writes beautiful haikus to summarise the events of the day and also has a wonderful sense of humour. Here is the first haiku he sent to us:
Mud, mud everywhere...
Hey, this place looks pretty good!
The start begins here!

Louis Lane

She is a journalist in the UK with a great deal of NGO experience. She rolls the media machine and helps our stories get published including on Al-Jazeera. Her work is invaluable. She is a stand-up comedian in her part time but more importantly, she keeps our feet firmly on the ground.

The Ottoman Cooks

There are four Turkish Doctors Worldwide team members. 2 are doctors, 2 are paramedics / search and rescue specialists. I can only communicate with one. I have just begun implementing a role they can play in this mission and have today sent them with some interpreters to the static clinic we are rebuilding to see patients as our local doctor will have the day off. They will become part of our mobile team as soon as we put together a safe and suitable itinerary with logistical support. We are hoping to start a healthcare education programme of which they will play a big role in distribution of aid.

They are wonderful people and eat beautifully. Even in the hotel, they insisted on cooking their own food and even bought supplies from Turkey. We sit and eat together and have now started laughing together. I am very hopeful they will make a very positive impact now that our objectives have accommodated them. They have offered me a Turkish bride but Indiana Jones is too busy looking for the holy grail.

The Pakistani Support

I cannot thank my friends and others in the region whom have helped, although I have no code names, Farooq, Zeeshan and Faraz have all helped significantly in their own way. I have now begun learning how to delegate not just to our team, but also utilise the wonderful support we have here by the local people.

The Newcomers

More doctors are arriving. I do not know what talents and challenges they will bring to our team.

I would just like to thank this small team whom have done an amazingly wonderful job. We visited the hospital Medecin Sans Frontier have taken over in Nowshera, and although we are just miniscule compared to their size and we only recently started, our work parallels theirs significantly. In some ways, I believe our achievements are an improvement to what they are also achieving.

I am very proud of this team of what we have and can still do.

With love always,
Indy

17.08.2010 – Of Life And Death

Dear Readers,

Our project is bursting into life. From an unlikely trio, we have now become an eclectic mix of international volunteers and local staff. Our numbers now exceed over twenty and the complexity of our mission increases by the minute. Each contributor to our greater good has a significant role to play but also has their unique and specific needs which they naturally prioritise above all else. It is becoming more apparent to me that my position is now to try and keep all these colourful threads together to form a strong and beautiful rope that will hopefully help lift some of the Pakistani people out of the floods and their misery.

It is for this reason that I am seriously considering staying for another two weeks to help this splendidly stuttering machine move forward whilst our wheels are frantically being put on in true Pakistani style – by juggar! It is not the most glamorous position as I am often lumbered with some of the administrative or technical aspects of the project but if it allows the others' hard work to materialise, it is worth it. I have not been to the main clinic for two days whilst being stuck with paperwork and planning. Instead this has allowed the Turkish contingent an opportunity to thrive and thrive they have. On their first day on the site, they returned buoyant with pictures of the first child to be born in our clinic. I watched a video of the Turkish doctor reading an azan into the baby's ear as the Turkish team also proudly watched the footage, as the doctor explained how he helped deliver the baby. It was at this moment I believe, that our clinic too was born and a new hope for the Pakistani people began.

The Turkish team again returned today with wonderful pictures of their work ethic, distributing balloons to children as the doctors in the team performed our first minor operations – a drainage of a terrible abscess on a child's head and a removal of a foreign body from a man's foot. But as they cycled through their images of the day, they showed me some rather disturbing photos. It was that of a man, or rather, that of a corpse, clinging to his dear life with his left hand onto higher ground as the flood swept him under. As the river water now begins to recede, his body that had been under water for so long, has now become visible but still too dangerous to reclaim. Bystanders look helplessly on. And this for me has been the most striking reminder of why I as a person, Doctors Worldwide as an organisation, and we as the united world, are here supporting the people of Pakistan during what is a sobering and horrific event.

Today, I thanked the Turkish team for coming and told them I was happy they were here on our team and I also thanked them for cooking great food for us every day. I have also assigned an experienced doctor from Dubai who has just arrived to begin our mobile educational program and the Fantastic Mr Fox is organising a rather delightful food package for the poor and hungry in our region. We have now moved into our unfurnished house and office, leaving the hotel room behind from where we were running the show. I spent a long hour without electricity whilst sweating buckets staring at the ceiling fan just now, firstly wishing for the fan to start but secondly deciding whether I should stay or go. I think I need to stay to see the birth of a braver Pakistan but I cannot help but wonder how many dead are still clinging on under the flooded Pakistan.

Saqib

PS – My Urdu is coming along nicely but I have already kicked our football over the fence into the neighbours' garden (whilst teaching the Turks how to play of course) and I do not think I know how or have the confidence to say, "Please Sir, can I have my ball back"....

20.08.2010 – The Medicine Of Religion And The Religion Of Medicine

Dear Readers,

In our darkest and saddest moments, when it seems we have lost everything or there are no more viable solutions, the greatest medication of all seems to be that of religion and prayer. Even those with no religion or formalised belief system usually find something to cling on to that provides hope for the heart during difficult or impossible times.

I still remember the South African nurses singing Zulu hymns to their patients each morning, praying for a healthy recovery. And the paraplegic victims of the Haiti earthquake believing their God would allow them to walk again. And now during this Muslim holy month of Ramadan, I wonder how much strength it is giving to those now homeless as a result of the flood, living in tents or under the night skies with no worldly possessions, only their clinging faith in God. Prayer is an anti-depressant, an analgesic, a cure.

Last night I cried inside. Maybe it was because I have been witnessing the scale of the destruction of the floods on a daily basis for two weeks - the lines between normality, poverty and extreme poverty becoming increasingly blurry and confusing in my mInd. Or maybe I cried at the thought of the corpse that had been hanging on to its already lost life under a battered bridge we had driven past many times, unknowing that the dead too was also there travelling with us.

Or perhaps it was the thought of Fatimah, an extremely sick girl. Although we have saved her from death's door, she continues to be discharged from different government hospitals only one day after we refer her to them in a plea for her to be treated appropriately.

Or maybe it is the thought of the twelve-year-old girl with an abscess on her thigh that she has had for three months. The abscess has become so painful that she has not moved her knee for the same period of time. Her knee is now so horribly stiff in a bent position that she is unable to straighten it as she limps around malnourished, hopping and crying from chair to examination table and back to chair.

Or perhaps it is the thought of another baby girl that lost her life in her very first hours of belonging in this world as she too was transferred from one hospital to another looking in vain for a place that could save her. Her body, and we, as a nation failed her on her very first day of living

Or maybe I cried because of the scorching weather during this season of Ramadan is taking its toll. The punishing sun beats down unforgiving temperatures onto our bodies whilst we fast and sweat throughout the day, slowly losing our hydration before filling up when the sun eventually leaves us alone.

Or perhaps it is because of the electricity, this unreliable and cruel friend of mine, for every time it makes a heartfelt promise, it fails to deliver. My days and nights are spent occasionally without electricity and even as a I type this early in the morning, my friend still has not come home, leaving me to type in darkness and stifling midnight heat.

Or maybe I cried because of the despised cold showers that once worked have now become cold bucket showers as the amenities in our living quarters slowly begin to fail, just like the rest of Pakistan. Or maybe it was the thought of our Pakistani toilets and the utter discomfort of their design that broke my spirit last night.

Or perhaps it was my broken iPod, my trusted companion whose lullabies that have soothed me to sleep throughout my travels around the world. Now it crackles and hisses and pierces my ears. Or perhaps it is my laptop, whose fragile battery has been so electrocuted by the corruptly discharging Pakistani electricity it cannot function more than a few minutes on its own without failing me and losing my written work.

Or maybe it is the fact that I have extended my stay in Pakistan for two further weeks to enjoy all this a little longer. For I know that this small project that has now been started will likely stutter and splutter into a typical Pakistani failure unless there is some continuity of care, some dedicated focus and sustainable targets. Somehow I feel I need to be here longer to help see it through, to support those that will take the project further. It is for this reason I have stayed on for I refuse to be part of another effort wasted in this country.

Or perhaps, by staying two further weeks, I am upset because I miss out on a trip to Paris I had booked a while ago. And I was so looking forward to walking along the banks of the river Seine or visiting the Louvre to pacify my somewhat frazzled mind.

Yet through these difficulties I have just described, it is not the medicine of religion that gives me strength to carry on or hope that I can succeed. I do not turn to traditional religious prayer to guide me or give me belief. It is something entirely different that gives me my motivation – the religion of medicine.

It is this religion of medicine that gives me the power to stay focused, because this religion, the knowledge and understanding of medicine, gives one the ability to make important differences to the lives of others. And if one can make a difference, it gives lasting peace to those that accomplish it. Perhaps it is this religion's version of enlightenment. If Fatimah survives, or Shaista (the twelve-year old girl) walks again, I will have found my peace with God. I know the faster we work, the harder we work, the more efficient we are with the time we have, the more people (some of the poorest people in the world) will benefit from the small work we are doing and perhaps, as we have already proven, the more lives we will save.

It is therefore this religion, the religion of medicine that gives me the strength to carry on in such tiring conditions. I need no other medication.

With love always,
Saqib

PS –- Can someone keep me up to date with the Premiership football results please?

23.08.2010 – It is not Pakistan, it is Perishanistan

"Perishan" – Sadness
"Perishanistan" – The land of sadness

Dear Readers,

I have not seen myself in the mirror for over two weeks, I wonder how I look. All I feel is the hair on my face growing longer and more uncomfortable, almost in direct partnership with my unhappiness at the magnitude of the situation we are facing here.

I wonder, if I were to find a mirror and look myself directly in the eye, would my eyes be floating on hope over the flooded rivers of this land or would they sink under the water with the weight of despair. I have always lived by the belief that as humans, our love, our hope and our endurance can overcome any bridge, no matter how smashed it is. And throughout the simple trials of my life, I have always been proven wrong in this idealistic mantra. Now I fear for the people we are trying to help, I fear we cannot cross this bridge and I once again fear for my already battered ideals.

I was watching the pictures of the flood on the TV with my colleague in the first few days of arriving in the country, and he said something I really quite liked, "It is not Pakistan, it is Perishanistan."

It is not the floods directly that is overwhelming this belief. It is the previous 50 years, the previous 100 years, the previous lifetimes and generations of the people of this troubled land that worry me. It is the man-made disasters, the regional wars, the millions of refugees and internally displaced peoples that are hosted here. It is the natural disasters, the drought, the earthquake and the flood. It is the governmental instability and ineptitude of leadership. It is the rise and fall and rise of extremism. It is the growing population, the lack of education, the basic healthcare that is missing. It is the extreme poverty, its cycle and recycle. It is the lack of understanding, the lack of cooperation, the destruction of good will.

How do I tell our patients they deserve so much more than they ever got or are ever going to get? How do I tell the mother that just lost her newborn it did not have to be this way without hurting her? How do I tell the man that his condition should have been treated many years ago without hurting him more? How do I tell our dispensers not just to mumble the instructions of the medicines but to explain it thoroughly so the patient may understand the treatment when the dispensers do not understand this logic themselves? How do I ensure the patient understands the instructions when she cannot read or write? How can I tell my staff it is not acceptable for fifteen people to be in one crowded consultation room or that hygiene is of utmost importance, only for them to agree, solve the situation temporarily and return back to their ways when there is no supervision? How do I change the psyche of the Pakistani people after years of neglect?

And with all these questions, one continuously asks what are we trying to achieve here and can we be successful? Do we provide care for a day, a week, a month and leave, waiting for the next disaster to hit these poor people? Do we stay longer and if so, will the government assist or continue its rather ridiculous love story with drama and corruption?

Even the positive work by great people in this country is disorganised, chaotic and not always well thought out. If there were lessons to be learnt from the humanitarian relief aid from the previous earthquake in 2005, I doubt they have been learnt. I wonder if we are contributing to the chaos too. However, with all this confusion, I still have a small vision for our basic health unit with a fading sparkle in my eye. The same health clinic we found rotting in flood waters will hopefully rise to better than it ever was, for the short term and long-term use of the people it serves for years to come. And in this little, seemingly insignificant project, despite so many setbacks, I still have my hope.
With love always, Saqib

26.08.2010 – Sim Pakistani BHU (The Computer Game!)

Dear Readers,

For those that do not know me, I am a proud computer geek. I always have been a geek ever since my mother bought me NHS glasses with thick brown frames and lenses the width of jam jars when I was a little boy. And with this ridiculously short-sighted handicap, I began my adventure into the world of computers and their wonderful games. I immigrated from the Sinclair to the Amstrad to the Atari, Nintendo, Sega and eventually the PC.

Although my favourite games were always sports related, I developed a fascination for simulation games, spending hours upon hours sacrificing my youth playing games like Sid Myer's Civilisation, Railroad Tycoon, Theme Park and Sim City. The objective of these games was to develop an all-conquering organisation from scratch with absolutely minimal resources. In Civilisation, you would lead a civilisation to world domination starting from just a peasant, or Railroad Tycoon you would create a railway empire from one train or Sim City, one would try to create a world class city from just one building. In Theme Park, you would build rides and facilities for your visitors and monitor their happy or sad faces from their enjoyment of your park.

For the last three weeks of my life, it seems I have spent every minute and hour playing Sim Pakistani BHU (Basic Health Unit). The computer game's objective is to locate the site of a battered, flood smashed basic health care unit in Pakistan and rehabilitate it, rebuild the infrastructure, start treating patients, monitor their experience and with the knowledge gained from one BHU, expand the empire.

Now, in these simulation games, there is always the competitor whom you must compete against to provide the best service. In Sim Pakistani BHU, you are not competing with anyone but there are other players in the region, all trying to provide a health service. However, from the day I arrived, the emergency healthcare being provided was not the one I thought would offer the best impact for the people affected by the floods. All other service providers in the region were organising mobile health camps, where a health team of variable experience arrives in a van, locates an affected village or region for one day, chaotically (or sometimes well organised) reviews approximately one hundred patients, supply basic medications and then leaves for a new destination the next day.

The patients receive their medication in an often rushed or haphazard manner and there is no security or follow-up to know whether these medications are being taken properly or the conditions being treated are actually worsening. The players in the region are not coordinated from what I have seen and the patients of the region have no guarantees of if, when or where another mobile clinic might arrive. Asides from being slightly concerned of the efficacy of such treatment and whether good clinical medicine was being practised, I firmly believed from the start that although the mobile clinics have their uses as they could reach larger areas and reach people faster, they did not provide quality care in the short term or long term.

And so my game plan became the BHU Empire.

Now I am midway through the game and we have had some amazing successes. The word of mouth in the region is spreading about our service, just as we anticipated, and people as far as eight to ten kilometres are making their way to our static health care site for treatment and to be seen by our doctors. When initially fifty people came, now two hundred and forty people arrive. Visits from other NGOs completely agree with this philosophy and they are impressed with our work so far. Reports have suggested we are already functioning better than government BHUs in the region that were not even affected by the flood. Donors who come to see the work in progress are inspired, they donate more and our strength of service increases.

We are becoming established and we can expand, hoping to

provide more services, vaccination programmes are now being considered, maternity care, education programmes are potentially on the horizon.

And whilst other players rove around with the same mobile clinic philosophy, spot diagnosing, spot treating and leaving with no real contingency plan, we can now consider taking our service and expanding into other areas, thus establishing a primary health care facility that reaches out to these needy people right now and long into the future, perhaps helping to establish and promote other health centres that are struggling to treat the flood affected people.

However, there are still many hurdles in this game. I have not completed the water, electricity or sanitation mini-puzzles properly and so cannot move on to the next level. I leave you with my current game score.

Sim Pakistani BHU Score:

BHU Medication supply: 75% (Good stock, precarious supply chain). Status: BHU Journeyman

BHU Hygiene: 63% (Flood waters, mud, slime and swamps cleaned, clinical waste not managed well). Status: BHU Amateur

BHU Water: 77% (Water well pump, lifesaver jerry cans for clean water available, washing facilities and toilets not yet functional). Status: BHU Journeyman

BHU Electricity: 80% (Generator functioning, government electricity returning, still not 24 hours) Status: BHU Professional

BHU Medical equipment: 95% (Sats monitor, portable oxygen, nebuliser, tympanic thermometers (not seen before in region!). Status: BHU expert

BHU furniture:82% (Locked drugs cabinet, Hospital beds, patient screens, drip stands) Status: BHU Professional

BHU Patient numbers and satisfaction: 93% (Almost at full capacity, crowd control poor, but much better than last week).

BHU Staff:85% (Employing eight local staff members including doctor, dispensers and female nurse...lacking a female doctor, staff happy with progress). Status: BHU Professional

With love always,
Saqib

29.08.2010 – Heroes and Waving Goodbyes

Dear Readers,

The last letter I wrote before I left Haiti in February 2010 was titled "Heroes and Goodbyes". Although the title of this post is similar, I hope it will not be my final letter of this trip in Pakistan for there is still so much work to be done. I have been here for over three weeks and only have a few days left here before my minor contribution towards the relief of the Pakistani people comes to an end.

During this time, I have seen a simple idea grow from the depths of the dirty murky flood waters into a blossoming project. I have witnessed that even amidst the suffering of the affected and the chaos amongst those frantically assisting, logic combined with tireless passion can succeed.

The healthcare concept was simple. Firstly, do no harm by not providing a haphazard and clinically unsafe service. Secondly, to work within our resources and difficult circumstances to provide the best possible care to the most amount of people in a sustainable, controlled manner. Thirdly, to realise that our energy and work should not only contribute towards the short term relief of these deserving people but give them an opportunity to access improved basic healthcare long after the world has forgotten about them. Fourthly, to utilise the goodwill and contributions of our many supporters in a caring and constructive manner. Fifthly, to ensure we are working with agreement and permission from the local government. And lastly, with the possibility of growing resources and support, expand the concept urgently in collaboration with others.

We are rapidly moving towards the final objective. A memorandum of understanding signed with the relevant government officials has now allowed our organisation to work in two basic health clinics serving populations whose lives have been destroyed by the floods. Further discussions are taking place with other non-government organisations to urgently establish quality maternity care in these units as well as re-establishing a vaccination programme (for another baby boy was born on our site just two days ago). And I have been further approached by other organisations to export this ideology and experience we have gained to other affected areas further south, in Punjab and Sindh. And thus, by treating a symbolic few thousand patients well, we may soon be able to treat tens and hundreds of thousands of patients well.

Although it is only the first step of a proverbial thousand-mile journey, an identifiable footprint has been made into the mud left by the aftermath of the receding water. There is a real opportunity created here to make a long-lasting difference to the lives of the people here. But it will require tremendous strength, relentless energy,unprecedented organisation in disorganised Pakistan, luck blessed by God Himself, generous support and an undying passion for the people that need our help. In my brighter, more hopeful, more optimistic moments, I still believe it is possible.

And the reason I believe this vision is possible is that during my three weeks here, I have met many heroes, both from Pakistan and abroad. Indeed, I can count at least ten volunteers from the UK, Turkey and Dubai that have arrived after me and departed before me, contributing significantly in their own unique way to this project. Furthermore, another seven volunteers have just arrived, ready to begin their much-needed contribution. Beyond this, there have been countless wonderful people in Pakistan that have supported us to help us achieve what we have so far.

I have always lived by the philosophy that every human being I meet along my journey in life is my teacher. No matter if I personally enjoy or dislike their company, no matter if I agree or disagree with their thoughts or actions, every person will always have a quality or virtue better than mine that I can learn from to improve myself, whether it be an aspect of their personality or an aspect of their knowledge. And on this journey I truly have learnt so much.

I have been here three weeks and witnessed my heroes and

my teachers come and go. One of the greatest joys of living in this world is being able to meet these great and amazing people. And one of the greatest sorrows is having to wave goodbye.

With love always.
Saqib

03.09.2010 – The Ministry Of Corruption (And Its Associated Buffoonery)

Dear Readers,

The term institutionalised corruption suggests that corruption has slowly crept into the psyche of the Pakistani people and into its governmental institutions like a plague of insects, thoroughly rotting the once noble foundations before taking over the system like money sucking leeches. However this term seems rather mild in describing the current affairs in the country.

Rather than institutionalised corruption, it seems the country has an entire dedicated governmental Ministry of Corruption, which I term "the MoC". I believe this is a specialised, well-formed institution with policymakers specifically producing disorganised and illogical thinking. The MoC's objective is to encourage maximally effective corruption and promote the Pakistani brand of dishonesty, untrustworthiness and buffoonery throughout the entire world.

It has been so disheartening to have had the same conversation with every single Pakistani I have met, whether poor or rich, home or abroad, flood affected or flood relief workers. They do not trust the government to perform any task, simple or complex with any skill or integrity. Instead the people complain with vigour and rigour that the government will just swallow finances like a Venus money trap and place it into its own already bulging belly.

Although the Pakistani floods have affected more people than the tsunami and the Pakistani and Haitian earthquakes put together, the international response has been insignificant in comparison. The reason simply is that along with the people of Pakistan, the people of the world also do not trust the government. Instead, money has been seeping its way into the country through small, hand to hand donations and to non-governmental organisations working here that have a modicum of transparency and trustworthiness.

Initially I did not involve myself much in the people's conversations of complaints and grievances regarding the government's ineptitude. However, having witnessed some of the Ministry of Corruption's successful projects, I am compelled to join the Pakistani people in their whining through this latest letter.

When I arrived in the country from Birmingham, I was appalled to watch the President of Pakistan, Zardari make the exact opposite trip, travelling from Pakistan to Birmingham for predominantly social reasons whilst the country drowned in front of him. It was painful but also humorous to watch a shoe being thrown at him whilst he was in Birmingham on Pakistani television but less humorous to discover the TV channel that had shown it has been taken off air whilst the government denied the incident.

I was utterly flabbergasted to read that the Pakistani government had requested one of the UN offices (International Telecommunications Office) to place aid donations into an unmonitored Swiss bank account. Such outright and outrageous buffoonery is somewhat incomprehensible and suggests Pakistan's corruption is so rife it no longer has any shame.

I was at first disbelieving when local Pakistanis were telling me flood waters had been deliberately diverted away from certain lands in the Sindh province (by breaking infrastructure) to protect land and houses owned by influential and rich members of the government. And then my heart sank when the news has only just broken on the international media scene suggesting it is true.

And to consolidate its good work and destroy the morale of the Pakistani people further, the Ministry of Corruption has again successfully exported its Pakistani brand of stupidity onto the cricket team. The heroes of the Pakistani nation once again breaking the heart of the people by acting like the government – selfish, corrupt, greedy and without an ounce of pride for the people it represents. It's really sad when the only joy for these people in such tremendously difficult times is now another reason to feel dejected in more match fixing scandals.

For me personally, all these stories were news reports, media hype and second hand information. However I too was treated to a delightful display of Pakistani buffoonery a few days ago as I attempted to collect cargo from Islamabad airport that had been sent by one of our team members for our relief work. Pakistani International Airlines (PIA) and the government had offered free delivery and free customs of relief goods into the country. However, when I arrived at the airport, I was told that the goods we were expecting were now owned by PIA and our boxes would be making their way to the army without question. After some raised tempers and significant threats from my colleague, we were told to go back and have our paperwork changed by the UK office, who were by no means, innocent in this buffoonery.

Three days later I returned (by myself with a hired pickup truck) and with updated paperwork only to be told I needed further customs paperwork to collect the cargo. Their request (although extremely frustrating as this had not been mentioned on the previous visit) seemed genuine. After frantically organising the fax of the desired paperwork with some countless phonecalls and emotional pleas, I was treated to some more delightful Pakistani idiocy.

I witnessed my paperwork being transported to no less than six offices at different points in the airport. Within each office sat a man with a non-specific title who would firstly be busy with other clients, before musing over the paperwork and adding his signature. After six signatures were collected, the details are then placed onto at least 3 very old looking computer systems, all manned by computer technicians who are either not at their desk or seemingly too busy to acknowledge your presence.

After six hours at the cargo office, through a combination of incompetence at the UK office and downright institutionalised idiocy at the Pakistani office, I managed to collect nine out of our ten cargo boxes whilst also paying a hefty price for the so called free delivery of the relief goods. The last box is languishing behind, its fate uncertain and it's heart-breaking to know people's donations are left like this. The entire PIA cargo decks are filled with donations and supplies that the quite ridiculous system cannot cope with.

Internally I too am now seething at this government's actions and I have been here less than four weeks. I now understand why every Pakistani is so demoralised. But I always try to end these diaries with some hope. Firstly, I have been privileged to work with an exceptionally caring government official in the Nowshera district who has not only supported our efforts but has been working harder than us, something I thought harder to achieve within the government.

I have had four meetings with him, and each one of them has been just before midnight in his office, as we quickly drive down to meet him at the end of our day's work. Since arriving into the region after the floods, he has worked from eight am until midnight every day without fail and has won my trust as a man who does what he says with good intentions and good results.

And secondly, the good nature of the genuine people of Pakistan is still there and as long they remain, there is still hope in the country. In the KPK region, an area in which the local people are already overburdened by millions of Afghanistani refugees and internally displaced people as a result of the Taliban fighting, they are still doing what they can to help with the floods. They tirelessly deliver water, food and assist with organisations like the one I am working for. In the UK, I could never imagine us tolerating so many refugees, so many internally displaced people with such open hearts and then working as hard to battle both the government and natural disasters to help even more.

Despite the Ministry of Corruption and its associated buffoonery, there is still hope for Pakistan. And it lies within the hearts of these good people who still work so hard despite the ongoing nonsense described in this post.

With love always,
Saqib

03.09.2010 – The AJW Book Project

Dear Readers,

Great men and women are like the jewels of the earth. They are the precious stones, the diamonds, rubies, sapphires and emeralds that glitter in their own natural beauty and in their own wondrous, distinct colours. Whether they are seen or not by an admiring world, they will continue to shine just as bright.

And just like gemstones, the vast majority of these great people remain hidden within the Earth's crust, yet to be discovered, shielding their beauty from the outside, shining quietly in their own discrete light. It is these quietly dazzling people that are the most precious of our world's natural riches and resources.

I have debated internally a great deal whether to write this post about AJW. For you see, unlike me, great people do not write letters to the world about their own actions, thoughts, philosophies and internal ramblings. They do not seek attention or admiration and just like the diamond that is unwillingly cut and forced into the clasps of a metal ring or necklace to be put on display, I am wary not to do the same with the subject of this letter. It is for this reason I refer to this gemstone with my abbreviated nickname for him, AJW and not his full name.

I have spent four weeks with AJW and from him I have learnt a great deal about improvising, finding solutions and dedicating ones efforts to the lives of others. I have worked tirelessly with him, helping him run this project and driving up and down the country, making the most of every minute we had to be as productive as possible.

I remember us both falling asleep in the front of our Suzuki van whilst waiting in an Islamabad side street to pick up another generous donation, just minutes after hauling forty boxes of goodies into our van from the World Health Organisation office. And I remember when he was tiring at the wheel, he would ask me to properly pull the hair on his head to wake him up and when that did not work, I would take the wheel whilst he slept in the back.

I have seen him assist everyone that has asked him for help with complete willingness, often tiring himself out in the process. And yet as I too grew tired, welcomed by the thought of returning home, I realised AJW would be continuing to tire himself out for a lot longer after I had gone.

And this is not the first time he has been in this situation. He told me of the two years he spent in Afghanistan, working in a medical camp, showing me pictures of victims of the war being treated in very basic conditions. He described how he was unable to return home to be by his mother's side during her last dying days even as she called for him.

He told me how he was again helping with the victims of the earthquake when his wife gave birth to his son. He was informed all was well only to be told his son had died two weeks later. The first time he saw his newborn child was when he urgently returned home to bury him.

I was told by another colleague that whilst AJW was on duty with our organisation, there had been a fire at his family home, destroying his family's livestock and livelihood. He quickly went back home and upon returning to work, he was asked if everything was ok. He smiled and merely said, "Everything is fine, we just have a lot of roast chicken. Just not halal though".

The floods of 2010 totally destroyed his house. He has not had a chance to begin cleaning it up because of his commitment to our work. He still has not seen his family or baby daughter in four weeks, his daughter was only born one day before the floods began. When I visited his house, he told me sadly of his book collection that had been destroyed, a twenty-year collection of his most prized books.

It was at that moment, I decided to restart his book collection. However, proud and noble people in this culture do not easily accept gifts, especially if they are born out of perceived struggle and strife. Instead, I bought a gold leaf hardback book on the art of calligraphy (a passion of his), and had every one of the past and present volunteers sign it before they left as a token of our appreciation for all his work over so many years for the people of this region.

And so the AJW book collection has begun, I have left another hardback gift book on poetry for the next team to sign and give it to him on departure. One of the saddest moments leaving the country is not knowing if you will ever see such great people again, such glittering but hidden jewels of the earth.

With love always,
Saqib

06.09.2010 – Into The Past, The Present And Into The Future (The Last Two Letters)

Dear Nana, Dada, Dadi, Nani, (my grandparents)

I never knew you. I either met you during fleeting moments of my childhood or I met you through stories passed down by my parents. And yet it was only your memory alone that bought me back to this troubled land with such eager determination.

This year I was blessed to discover that many years ago you too had written diaries of living in this land now known as Pakistan. You described the unimaginable struggles of your lives, the hardships you faced and how your strength overcame them. You described the changing times of British India, the social and economic difficulties, the upheaval and uproar of the political instability. You described what life is like when you are homeless and penniless but more importantly, you described how life is when you are not hopeless, not loveless. Your writings were inspirational and beautiful to me.

And so during my own difficult times during this journey, it was thoughts of you that kept me going. In every hungry moment, I remembered your hunger. In every tired moment I remembered the thankless hours of manual work you did just to pay for a small meal. In moments of sadness, I remembered how you still succeeded.

But most importantly, in moments of utmost frustration, when I looked up and saw the lives of the people struggling around me, man, woman or child, I too saw your lives within theirs and it pushed me to try harder, that by being here with these people, I was still connected to you.

And so when I found the time, I visited your final resting places, as I promised myself I would. And I prayed you were happy, in peace high above the starry skies and in peace within the hearts of all those that still and will always remember you fondly.

With love always
Saqib

Dear Readers,

My journey in Pakistan has come to an end but the journey of
the medical project I have been involved with has only just
begun. In the context of these unprecedented floods along the
entire length of the seemingly all destroying Indus River, it is
merely a small project, assisting only a fractional percentage
of the vast populations whose lives have been so severely
affected.

But in the context of those small number of people that the
project is reaching out to, it really is a matter of life and death,
of fighting preventable disease, of improving battered lives
and livelihoods, of giving help and hope to the somewhat
hopeless and helpless.

Friends and family on my return have all commented on the
great work I have performed and yet it does not feel this way.
Indeed, the chairperson of Doctors Worldwide (a fellow
orthopaedic surgeon!) arrived in Pakistan the day before I left.
He also thanked me and commented on my personal
achievements during these tough times.

I denied that I or we had achieved anything yet. A project that
fails to realise its potential is not a worthwhile achievement no
matter how great or poor the start. The clinic we are running
is at a tipping point. It can either crumble if its supporting
foundations are removed or it can become stronger,
developing a solid grounding to provide vital care for these
impoverished people long into the future, long after I and we
all have forgotten about them. It will always need support and
energy, your support, my support and our collective energy for
many months if not years to come.

More volunteers from the UK have arrived and are working in
the field, taking the project further, dedicating their time and

love to the people of Pakistan. One of my regrets is not being with them to help the project blossom. My last request to the Chairman and the new team as I said goodbye was to make sure they go onto fulfil its purpose and truly become the great project it has the potential to be. They promised it would and I hope I will be able to keep you all updated on its positive progress some day in the future.

As I made my final way to Islamabad airport, the driver I had worked with for four weeks mentioned how every one of the local staff members was sad I was leaving. I asked him why, mentioning that there was a whole new team to keep them busy. He answered by saying it was because I knew everyone and everyone knew me. I did not fully understand this but it reminded me of a time when a student nurse in South Africa described me as having the Zulu word for humanity. It was another comment I did not quite understand.

I do not believe there is such a thing as true altruism. And truthfully, my motives are purely self-serving. In a time of floods and earthquakes, of wars and suicide bombings, of visible famines and diseases on TV, of extreme poverty and inexplicable injustice against the innocent, I am merely acting to find my place and peace within this strange world.

In a world where its people would rather seek more comfort for themselves at the expense of others, where its people exploit the minor differences between themselves rather than embrace our overwhelming similarities, my motives are merely to try and understand why this is so. If by chance, my actions help or improve the lives of others, it is simply a side effect of my personal quest to belong in a world I still do not understand.

I did not always display my writings so frivolously. They are truly only written for me. As a child, as a teenager and as an adult, I would write and release the words trapped in my head and heart, happily throwing them away, emptying the space, ready for the next batch of invading words.

I was only recently convinced by someone to display some of these writings for some equally crazy people in this world who may want to read them. And so, for those readers that have joined me on this journey, and those that have responded with the countless messages of support whilst writing these letters, I am truly thankful and humbled by your support. My words would not be able to explain my gratitude.I am hopeful however, that in the future, there will be a day I no longer need to write such long-winded explanations, that I can quietly go about my way without such ramblings. I am hopeful it will be the day I too will have found my peace,

With love always,
Saqib

Cambodia (2013)

By 2011, I had commenced a trauma and orthopaedic training programme in my home city of Birmingham, UK. The programme is designed to last for six years, rotating through numerous local hospitals on six monthly placements. The ultimate objective is to complete specialist examinations in the field of trauma and orthopaedics (FRCS Tr& Orth), whilst simultaneously learning essential practical skills and preparing for the trials of being an independently practicing surgeon.

At the start of the rotation, all new programme starters were told taking time out of the programme would not be advisable. Although my previous experiences abroad had inspired me to focus on orthopaedic surgery in low and middle income countries, I settled down to complete my six-years of training before entertaining any future projects abroad. I was determined to be as qualified to the highest standard if I ever wanted to contemplate treating patients ethically in a less developed nation.

However, in 2013, whilst genuinely focussing on the programme within the UK, I received a message on Facebook from an old British colleague whom I worked with in South Africa. He was in Cambodia, on a paid fellowship at the Children's Surgical Centre (CSC), Phnom Penh. He explained no one else had applied for the next fellowship and he wondered if I would be interested in going.

The Facebook message simply read as follows, "Saqib, there maybe a job going in Cambodia starting in August for six months. Quite a lot of managerial experience as well, would you be interested?"

Without hesitation, I immediately made enquiries and pleaded with my programme director to make an exception and allow me six months away from the programme. Indeed, with further paperwork, I managed to obtain educational approval for the fellowship from the Royal College of Surgeons. And so, without further ado, I travelled to Phnom Penh, to work at a charitable centre providing free surgical treatment to the impoverished people of Cambodia.

18.05.2013 – Surgery On The Shoulders Of Giants

Dearest Readers,

My last medical diary entry, in 2010, left Pakistan in floods. My final words were of a promise, that I would stop writing when I had found my peace amidst the perpetual chaos and seemingly incessant trauma of this world. I have been working in Cambodia now for three months and yet I have been silent with no significant outpouring of words, thoughts, emotions, and of course, no awkward letters that have always kept me company along my very own awkward, stumbling travels.

However (and unfortunately), this silence has not been because I have found a lasting peace in this land of a thousand (truly) genuine smiles. The silence is a manifestation of a frazzled mind. As the elixir of this beautiful country slowly drips into my blood and is propelled passionately through my veins by my beating heart, it also infiltrates and invades my head, jarring it into a speechless, expressionless stupor. Surgery in Cambodia is an immense challenge, intellectually, physically, emotionally and ethically.

Surgery here has pushed boundaries within me that I thought had already been swept aside by my past experiences. I have now been left scrambling for cover under those previous memories for comfort and safety. Often at night, after a challenging day of surgery, I reminisce and gain strength from those crazy moments along my past journey and I remember the heroes of my travels that have inspired me to now be standing in Cambodia somehow.

And so my first letter from Cambodia is a tribute to those giants of my past, those that installed the pillars of strength in this frayed mind and the reason why I remain positive, productive and still hopeful in these immensely challenging circumstances.

So, I am thankful to Dr Paul Rollinson, in South Africa, who taught me calmness amongst absurdity, who taught me patience and perseverance when it was easier to lose your temper. He taught me that leadership did not mean being loud. He taught me what one could achieve with a lifetime in surgery and how to do it.

And so I am thankful to Carwyn Hill, in Haiti, who taught me how desire, commitment and passion could truly achieve the seemingly impossible in ridiculously difficult circumstances. He taught me giving is the greatest gift one can receive. And he taught me the truest meaning of kindness and it has remained with me. He taught me heroism did not mean acting like a hero.

And so I am thankful to Abdul Wahab, in Pakistan, who taught me that every problem had a solution and that where there is a will, there is a way. From calamity to disaster to calamity, he taught me to keep rising, to keep fighting, to move forward to the next challenge, with all the solutions ready in your top pocket and a smile on your face!

So I am a surgeon on the shoulders of these giants, who still carry me forward when I feel like dropping in the confusion of it all. And I realise these memories are some of my greatest valuables in my life.

I have often said that hope is the most valuable currency, for hope is worth more than all the gold in the world. A rich man with no hope is far poorer than a poor man with bright eyes. But now I realise, with this currency of hope, one must purchase beautiful memories.

Our most valuable treasures that remain with us are our memories of the past. The man with the happiest memories now becomes the richest in the world for a poor man with a wonderful past is at more peace than a rich man with unhappy memories to keep him company at night. We go to sleep with our treasured memories and we wake up with our currency of hope, ready to purchase more happy memories.

And so now in Cambodia, I remain hopeful and working diligently to create more beautiful memories, more epic moments, more golden treasures that I will hold onto, long into my life. I am no longer investing in my future as the mantra goes, but investing in my past. My next letters will detail the incredible memories I am saving for myself, if I can wake from the frazzled mind and Cambodian induced stupor!

With love always,
Saqib

27.05.2013 – Phay Samnang*

Dearest Readers,

When I graduated from Nottingham University Medical School in 2004, I would never have imagined my medical journey would lead me to the inland and remote villages of Cambodia, looking for a boy called Phay Samnang.

As I set out that bright morning along dusty roads with some members of hospital staff (a driver, a translator and a keen medical student), with minimal information on the boy, just an age, a village name and a diagnosis in 2002 of osteosarcoma (bone cancer), I thought this was perhaps the strangest activity I had ever performed as a doctor.

The search for Phay Samnang was part of a bigger project, a study on the outcomes of osteosarcoma, a tragic form of bone cancer that often strikes in the pearls of youth, just as we are beginning to understand the world, form opinions, build beautiful relationships, begin to dream and fall in love. Even in the western world, the diagnosis of osteosarcoma is a hammer blow, with latest advances in treatment still confining the patient to an epic battle of chemotherapy and surgery to save their limb and life.

And tragically still, in Cambodia, this battle of osteosarcoma is even more dangerous, with fighting raging on all fronts - the struggle highlighting deficiencies in the Cambodian healthcare in every aspect. Those Cambodians, poor and often uneducated, do not seek medical opinion at the slightest swelling or pain in their bones. They would carry on in their humble lives, in hopeful neglect, like many of us often do when faced with a minor illness that our cumbersome symptoms will resolve on their own. And even when the swelling worsens, and the pain deepens, patients in Cambodia would often ignore their worries to concentrate on that very important activity of earning money to live and support a family.

Those that eventually seek help will often look for guidance from a traditional healer, placing their faith in the medicine of their forefathers. And those that seek more contemporary medical advice will too commonly find they cannot afford even the simplest investigations such as x-rays and blood tests. The government hospitals too, carry charges that are unaffordable.

And so the swelling grows, and the pain worsens and the worries of the patient gather. They hear of our free-for-all centre, and with swellings the sizes ranging from tennis balls to footballs, present to us in the latter skirmishes of an already raging war within them, very advanced and often too late. With little weapons to assist, we often advise an amputation to prolong life and perhaps, the slimmest chance of even cure, with the additional use of limited chemotherapy, again a costly process offered by local oncologists. And yet the prospect of an amputation in Cambodia, for these young patients is akin to a lifelong imprisonment and hearing such news, would often disappear back into the medical wilderness from where they came, perhaps hoping they never sought advice in the first place.

Our study was to research the outcome of almost forty such patients who had come for help in their war with osteosarcoma over the last twelve years. Some had opted for surgery, others lucky enough to obtain chemotherapy, whilst others refused treatment altogether, preferring the bleakness of their prognosis to the bleakness of difficult treatments. Bone cancer in Cambodia is a difficult condition, our study aims to highlight just how difficult it has been over the recent years.

And so I travelled along dusty roads, with no photograph, no next of kin, to a remote village many hours' drive away, looking for a boy who arrived at our centre eleven years ago at the age of eighteen, in 2002. He came with a horrendously large tumour around his knee and he was a brave patient, for he opted for an amputation. The hospital lost contact with him shortly after the operation. I was not sure what answers I was looking for, my data told me he was eighteen, but had he survived, he would surely be almost thirty now.

I could not imagine finding him on such limited data from so long ago. It was a search like I had never experienced. There were no telephone directories, no internet searches, no national or local government records to refer to. After a long journey, we arrived at a central village commune with a piece of paper in our hand displaying just a name, an age and a village name, along with a story of him presenting to our hospital in 2002. To me, it felt absurd that I was even looking, in the middle of Cambodian nowhere.

The middle-aged commune administrator, somewhat surprised by the appearance of a foreign doctor, a medical student and two random hospital staff, was remarkably calm with our somewhat ambitious mission to find Phay Samnang.

He pulled out his glasses, peered at us quizzically, sat us down at a rickety wooden table and opened a book with a list of twenty-three telephone numbers of all the local village leaders, each a potential source of the knowledge we were looking for. He fished out his old Nokia phone from his pocket and began slowly dialling the first on the long list of numbers. His voice cleared, and he began a conversation in Khmer that I soon became very familiar with and practically internally memorised.

I am pretty sure it translated into:

"I am looking for Phay Samnang, he went to the hospital in KienKlang (the district in Phnom Penh where our clinic is located). He had an amputation in 2002".

The conversation always ended fairly quickly thereafter, with a rattle of nods and mostly shakes followed by a disconnection of the phone call. The administrator would then proceed to the next number on the list and the agonisingly repetitive process would begin again as the search continued.

As helpless bystanders, we all donated our phones to the effort, each of us pre-inputting the next phone number on the list of village elders and having our phones ready for the administrator to dial as soon as the expected negative answer came from the last phone call. I sat there, somewhat dazed by this process, shaking my head in the heat and wondering what I was hoping to achieve here, hours away from where I had begun the day.

The process continued and the numbers left on the list dwindled. The team I was with became increasingly forlorn, decreasingly hopeful, anticipating our quest would end with no answer, an outcome I suspected from the moment we set out.

At the twentieth phone call and familiar conversation and familiar end of conversation, suddenly one of the other phones involved in our multi-phone dialling mission started ringing back. The administrator answered it and proceeded to a longer conversation, more nodding this time than shaking of the head, a stern frown, before passing the phone to our hospital staff. The rest of us became silent, an unlikely combination of concern and hope crept upon our faces as we intently listened.

The phone call ended a few minutes later, with the translator telling us the village elder from one of our phone calls had found Phay Samnang's mother. We subsequently drove to her humble abode. She tearfully recounted her son's story, that he attended our clinic in 2002, had an amputation and went home shortly after. He was unable to afford chemotherapy. His battle ended five months later, dying at home. Her mother told us he was in significant pain in the last two months of his life. She thanked our staff for the efforts of the clinic, reassuring us that we had correctly informed her of the patient's diagnosis and prognosis (a communication barrier that often exists between patient and hospital in the developing world). She knew everything that was possible had been made possible.

And there ended the story of Phay Samnang. A story that stuck with me on the more respectful, more silent, sombre journey home, dawning upon me a realisation of the difficulties, the challenges, the sometimes-unwinnable battles that we all must face. A realisation that those in this beautiful country of Cambodia must battle harder, battle longer, battle stronger than I could ever imagine before I arrived.

The episode left me with a belief that what we are looking for can be found, if we remain patient enough and look long enough. But sometimes we may find answers we were secretly not wishing for.

With love always and deepest respect,
Saqib

*Name changed for confidentiality reasons

08.06.2013 – The Rise And Fall, The Fall And Rise

Dearest Readers,

Cambodia is enchanted and cursed by a mesmeric, tumultuous history. The city of temples, Angkor Wat, is the spiritual Kingdom within the country and still reigns over camera-clad tourists and orange-robed pilgrims alike, all bowing together from around the world. The temples rose majestically in the twelfth century, becoming and remaining to this day, the largest religious site in the world. Angkor Wat is a fusion of Hinduism, Buddhism, epic stone architecture and iconic now-beheaded deities. It was the capital of the Khmer empire, a powerful South East Asian regime that gradually fell from grace over the following centuries.

The Khmer fell into decline thereafter, losing its land and influence to neighbouring empires and entered a period known as the Dark Ages, although an even darker age was soon to follow. Colonialism began in earnest in 1861, as Cambodia fell under the protection of France and soon merged with other French colonies to become an often ignored and neglected part of the French Indochina. A fleeting Japanese invasion and four-year occupation through World War II and growing anti-French sentiment led to declaration of Cambodian independence in 1953.

A period of Royal power, democratic uncertainty and relative prosperity alongside growing corruption commenced whilst its neighbour, Vietnam transformed into a battlefield of a war fought between more powerful nations. The war and instability in Vietnam toppled over into Cambodia, eventually leading to the rise of the Khmer Rouge in 1975, a fanatical communist regime and the start of the even darker age – perhaps the darkest age.

The Cambodian genocide was a systematic destruction of the architecture of the country's society and led to the death of over two million people in a four-year period. It is estimated

127

this human catastrophe resulted in almost fifty-percent of the Cambodian population losing their lives. Every Cambodian today has been affected by this tragic period.

And yet even after the defeat by the Khmer Rouge by Vietnamese forces, the country remained in the wilderness for many years thereafter, as internal wrangling, foreign neglect and the loss of a generation took its toll. It is only over the last twenty years that Cambodia has begun to slowly rise again, crawling up from its knees. There are elections at the end of the month, and although the political system is rife with corruption and instability, there is a verve and excitement among the people here, rallying and marching on the streets of Phnom Penh to display their political allegiance. The people are excited, hopeful and determined for a better future.

And so as Cambodia has fallen, risen, fallen and is rising again, so do the patients that present to our hospital. They come with terrible symptoms following familiar stories of injury or disease that has been neglected or incompletely treated in their past. They come with a hope that they may improve, that their infection can be cleared, that their tumour can be excised forever, that their bones can be fixed, that they can walk again, work again and be whole again. But sadly, medicine and surgery is not so simple.

And so as patients in Cambodia fall and hope to rise again, so do the surgeons that work in the hospital because treating such terrible pathology is fraught with dangers, pitfalls and unpredictable outcome. As the patient reaches up, wishing to climb up again, the surgeon may not have the resources to successfully lift that patient up. And as the surgeon lends out their hand, they too are in real danger of dropping the patient further and too, dropping down in despair with them.

Such are the difficult cases seen in the hospital that indeed, no surgeon in the world could always predict good outcomes and more often than not, it is easier to successfully predict bad outcomes. Surgery always carries a risk; there are no promises, no guarantees and in the face of such severe pathology, one must be willing to take bigger risks then I have previously been used to.

The knowing surgeon must therefore mentally cope with the outcomes of the surgical decisions he or she makes, decisions which ultimately are permanent, performing operations that the patients physically live with forever. I too have struggled with such burdens, knowing that I cannot always restore the patient to the path they want to be on or the path they should have been on had their pathology not been so badly and woefully neglected. I remember a case of a man with a severe infection in his tibia (shin bone), in which we tried on multiple occasions to surgically eradicate his infection only for us to eventually fail as the man eventually gave up on treatment for he could no longer afford to stay away from his family. And in the end, he lost his leg. But there have been many surgical successes too, and I have been privileged to be involved in those cases that led to better lives.

And so, as Cambodia continues to rise following its tragic and epic history of falls, I too must rise from the mistakes I have made in my past, from the falls I have sustained along my journey, from those unforgiving moments when I have failed myself and others.

I am inspired from this land to remain hopeful, to keep trying, to keep believing, that no matter how hard I fall, I must rise and I will rise. I will rise.

With love always,

Saqib

10.07.2013 - The Infinite Optimism Of Tuk Tuk Drivers

Dearest Readers,

Tuk tuks are intricately carved wooden wagons powered by underpowered, rattling motorcycles. They are the most common form of public transport in Phnom Penh, colourfully decorating the streets, chugging endlessly through the smog and smoke of the city whilst transporting Cambodians and tourists alike from one secret destination to another. They are often full to the brim, and occasionally, over the brim as people cram in like a human jigsaw to economise on this beautiful and wonderfully cheap method of transportation.

Each tuk tuk is unique, ranging from basic wooden flooring and fading seating pattern to those with lush leather interiors and gaudy trinkets hanging and swinging from the roof. Occasionally you will come across an eccentric tuk tuk, decorated like the bat mobile or with an epic sound system installed, blurting Khmer dance music with the confused occupants laughing and smiling at equally confused onlookers.

Every ride in a tuk tuk is an incredible adventure as friendly drivers will usher you into their chariots and negotiate amicably a fare for the anticipated journey. The cheeky ones will try to overcharge you but if you glance at them sternly, hidden behind an open smile and with a shake of the head, the driver will soon know his game is up. He returns too with a broad smile and negotiates more realistically a fair price. Following this, there is the confusion of actually determining where your final destination is as most drivers nod their head with complete confidence and knowledge of where you are going, before zooming off frantically and energetically in the wrong direction.

Furthermore, there is the vibrant, vivid stimulation of the journey as the sights, sounds and smells of this crazy city imbibe their way into the tuk tuk. One cannot help but watch the incessant activity bristling on every corner, people going about their daily lives. The scenes of Phnom Penh, as seen from a tuk tuk, are deserving of their own letter, such is the magnitude of the city's charm.

The tuk tuk drivers themselves are a beautiful, eclectic mix of wonderful people. Although incredibly poor, earning a mere few dollars a day on average, they will reliably offer a warm smile and wave whenever and wherever you are walking through the city. And despite their continual search for more passengers in a city bustling with competing tuk tuks, they have a deep and honest respect for each other with a knowledge and understanding of fairness when finding their clients. I have never personally seen a conflict amongst drivers, almost as though there is a secret, unwritten code amongst them that defines their etiquette and working relationship.

There is a group of tuk tuk drivers stationed outside my apartment that are my favourite people in the world. They are a mix of young and old drivers, descending from all corners of the Cambodian heartlands and fate somehow has brought them together on to my street. They wait all day in the stifling sun, neatly parked in their row of tuk tuks, patiently hoping for the next client to emerge from the surrounding apartments and coffee shops. They will always greet me with a heartfelt, genuine smile and wave happily to me as I sleepily crawl out on to the streets in the morning on the way to work. It is truly an incredible way to start your day, in contrast to the solitude of growling and driving to work in England, never acknowledging another human being's existence on your journey.

I will often watch this lovely group of tuk tuk drivers from my balcony above as they animatedly interact with each other before all sitting down together to eat simple meals on their makeshift tables and chairs. There is a real palpable camaraderie between them and I often secretly wish I was down there too, living my world in the comfort of their friendships, laughter and the sharing of the daily grind with one another. I will occasionally wander off to the local convenient store and buy them all drinks at their mealtime to somehow be a part of their friendship, and as they thank me with warmness, I wish I could just say in Khmer, "I want to be a tuk tuk driver too".

And yet my favourite aspect of tuk tuk drivers is their continual quest for passengers. You can walk along a busy street, lined with multiple tuk tuks and frequently hear their inquisitive call from behind you "Tuk tuk sir?".

You will turn your head back, smile, shake your hands negatively and say no. You will then turn your head forward to see yet another tuk tuk driver in front of you, who has just seen you reject one offer from a tuk tuk and offer you the same question, "Tuk tuk today sir?" with the largest welcoming grin, despite it being patently obvious you are walking to your destination.

You will smile once again and reject the offer. You will then bump into the third and the fourth driver, who has also witnessed your intention to walk and repeat the same question. You will start shaking your head and laugh wildly, amazed that the drivers will still hope to convince you to take their offer. Some might find this a very frustrating and tedious process, to continually reject these smiling people, but to me, it represents a beautiful optimism, that after one more offer, they may somehow convince you to finally jump in.

And sometimes, just sometimes, this eternal hopeful optimism of the offer, despite numerous rejected offers in the previous few seconds, convinces me I should jump on board, even if my destination is a mere simple walk away.

"Yes", I say, "Yes, today I will take your tuk tuk and your brand of infinite optimism",

With love always,
Saqib

15.07.2013 – The United Nations Of Medicine

Dearest Readers,

An anatomy textbook reveals the same insides of every human being on this planet - the solid muscular foundations between our bones and joints, the intricate, wired connections from our brain to our most distant nerves and the synchronous, beating partnership between our heart and lungs.

A physiology textbook explains how all of our bodies work - how breath gives us life, how blood flows through us, carrying our love through our heart and how we move with purpose, how we speak with distinction, how we see the beauty in the world, how we feel with the insides and outsides of our skin.

And travelling through this amazing world reveals the same human emotions in every land, the human condition that unites us all wherever we are - the condition where there is no true textbook. The world is filled with beautiful smiles during heartfelt moments, the colourless tears of sorrow when faced with anguish, the hope of brighter days, the anger of predictable injustice, the random kindness of strangers and the ultimate yearning to be loved and belong in a life that we all struggle to understand.

However, it is the pathology textbook that varies from land to land, for pathology describes how our bodies break and how it struggles and fights to repair. And although we are born with the same anatomy, the same physiology and with the same love in our heart and tears in our eyes, it is our environments that ultimately dictate how we break and for how long. Our access to healthcare is so phenomenally different, so imbalanced and so skewed, the pathology in the developed world is a completely different textbook to those less privileged. It is this disturbing difference that is so hard to tolerate. As I write these very words, those with imminently preventable disease are being ignored, those that are hungry are developing disease of malnourishment, those with simple surgical problems are being neglected, developing into complex, irreversible surgical conditions.

Although I have worked in one centre in Cambodia, I have witnessed and been a part of the truly United Nations of medicine in an attempt by those from around the world to help correct some of this global imbalance in pathology. Surgeons and healthcare professionals from near and far have come to assist at this small centre, contributing their wealth of knowledge and experience in assisting the staff here and treating those patients neglected by this worldwide injustice.

From all six corners of the USA, from Japan, from Hong Kong, from Singapore, from Australia, from New Zealand, from the UK, from France, from the rest of Europe, volunteers have flocked to this small centre and united their energy and effort to improve one life at a time, in this united nation of medicine. And from our shared knowledge of anatomy, our shared knowledge of physiology and our shared belief in the human condition, that we are all equal, that we all deserving, that we are all beautiful, we work together to improve the pathology that separates us all.

I have learnt so much from these volunteers, from senior surgeons to medical students, just beginning their life into medicine. I have been inspired by their enthusiasm, their energy, their wisdom and I am truly blessed to be part of this United Nations of medicine, one I will strive to always be a part of and that maybe one day, we can all too share the same pathology textbook and help each other overcome diseases together.

With love always,
Saqib

02.08.2013 – Sometimes There Are No Words

Dearest Readers,

I wanted to write with all my heart so regularly, about the adventures I have had in the last six months, about the glorious people I have met in this enchanted corner of the world, about the memorable stories I had gathered and the lessons I had learnt from my meandering, jangling, clumsy footsteps.

I usually write to release the catapult of thoughts building within me, thoughts I can never seem to speak and writing these letters fire these gathering boulders of words over the boundary walls guarding my speech and out into the freedom of the grasslands beyond me. I can then find these boulders of words later, in the rubbles of my past thoughts, a historical wreckage of writings, an indecipherable and ancient script that I can study again when I am a grey bearded historian and I can criticise its author for its confusing jargon and silly inaccuracies.

But sometimes there are words that can neither be said nor written, words that get trapped within you, somewhere lodged between your head and heart, deep down in your throat, somewhere the catapult cannot find them. And as I leave this beautiful land and make my journey home, I realise there are still so many trapped words within me.

Sometimes there are no words to express your gratitude to those people that have made you feel so welcome, so warm and so special, people that made you feel like you always belonged with them, even in a place you had never been before. And as the staff at the surgical centre said farewell on my last day, there were no words to tell them part of my heart belonged to them.

And sometimes there are no words to capture the truly remarkable sights, sounds, smells of a thriving, bustling, hilarious city and as I tried one last time to catch those words, driving around in my beloved tuk tuk, I realised I could never capture the beauty I saw on those streets in these past months.

And sometimes there are no words to say goodbye to new friends but a hearty handshake or an awkward hug followed by a hopeful wave, that they will always be safe, happy and healthy.

And sometimes there are no words to say goodbye to a long lost beautiful friend except to silently wipe her tears away and pray for another hello.

And sometimes there are just no more words.

With love always,
Saqib

05.08.2013 – The Return Home Again

Dearest Readers,

I have returned, travelling back from East to West, travelling from a far-away land to my home again.

And I have learnt that as the world is getting smaller, my small world is drifting wider apart and dividing me in two.

I have seen the widespread discrepancies in our planet, the poor and the rich, the struggling and the thriving, the hopeless and the hopeful and I have become surer of my purpose within it, to somehow narrow this gap, even if it means getting caught, helplessly trapped within this divide, suffocating within it.

I have seen a school that was once built for teaching, used for relentless torture. And I have visited fields dedicated for killing, thousands upon thousands of skulls stacked up into a pyramid, representing the extent of extreme cruelty that can exist in man's bones.

I have seen men, women and children carry bravely on, tolerating disease and injury as if it was a part of life, seeking help only when help sought them. And I have struggled to assist- emotionally, ethically, intellectually, physically in their plight, knowing that in another parallel universe, with more facilities, more equipment and better services, those lost dreams could be recovered so much more. It has burdened me, as have my on-going mistakes.

But I have worked in a centre filled with incredibly talented staff – hard working, motivated, loving and joyful. And I have been humbled to be a part of their team and made to feel I always belonged there, like I had been there my whole life.

And I have admired surgeons from around the world donate their time, expertise and love freely, willingly to form a united nation of medicine, where we are all equal and all one.

I have wandered the peaceful streets of a city with a tragic history and found a smile on every corner. And I have visited pagodas, temples, mosques and churches in an eastern land of warm, tolerant people.

I have drifted on a river, under soothing starlight music and discovered a thousand fireflies brighter than the stars above. And felt her light in my arms.

I have floated overnight in a majestic sea of two thousand limestone islets, seeking God's nature and prayed for a happy long lost childhood. And I have sought my fortunes from wise-eyed tellers and red packets full of promises.

I have dreamed about a giant rubber yellow duck that brings peace and unity across the world and I found it, stationed in a city of skyscrapers made of illusions and concrete mazes with beautiful secret spots made of Ribena kisses.

I have visited the largest religious site in the world, mystified by its ancient wisdom, astounded by its ancient carvings and watched the sun set over it with magical rays.

I have hiked close to waterfalls but dare not venture under them for fear of soaking completely and crushing my soul.

I have bussed, hopped and flown onto neighbouring islands, catching sand in my toes, sunlight in my eyes and ate on beaches and piers with Buddha views.

I have bussed, hopped and flown into neighbouring cities with family and friends, migrating through the smog of traffic and the traffic of smog to find delightful spots of cultural significance, museums, art exhibits, theatres, lakes of returned swords, night markets, high spots in skyscrapers and hill retreats and modern comforts in endless malls, friendly hotels and rooms of companions.

I have palpated my heart, beating softly again, cycling with it
on my sleeve and carving it for keeps in an old oak tree,
playing it for always on a hand painted wooden gramophone.

With love always,
Saqib

Ethiopia (2016)

In February 2016, I was delighted to have completed my FRCS (Trauma and Orthopaedics) examination. It was perhaps the most gruelling examination I had ever undertaken and for a brief moment in time, I felt bursting with knowledge that I knew my mind would not contain forever.

A few months later, World Orthopaedic Concern (WOC UK), an organisation dedicated to the development, teaching and training of orthopaedic surgery in the developing world, requested a training surgeon to accompany a senior consultant to visit Addis Ababa for two weeks. The purpose of the visit was to establish stronger links with the Black Lion Hospital, a teaching hospital in Ethiopia with a bustling orthopaedic training programme. Our role was to train the orthopaedic residents on a daily basis, imparting any clinical and surgical acumen we could to help them develop.

The World Orthopaedic Concern has had a historic and fruitful relationship with the Black Lion Hospital for many years, although recently the strong connection had somewhat faded. Efforts were being made to rekindle this strong bond, and our visit was also in effort to promote this new relationship.

I had also completed a post graduate certificate in medical education and felt I had the suitable skills and experience to volunteer. However, I was acutely aware that I already had many wonderful experiences and memories abroad, and I did not want to take an opportunity away from any colleagues that also wished to travel. I therefore made myself available but only if no other candidates became suitably available.

In May 2017, I flew out with a consultant to Addis Ababa. Neither of us had visited the Black Lion Hospital before, and naturally apprehensive of what to expect or what we might achieve in such a short visit.

14.05.2016 – Green, Yellow And Red Balloons

Dearest Readers,

I once wrote that I would stop writing when I had negotiated a peace, an acceptance of the world around me, a comfortable belonging and a secure place within it. And indeed, it has been a few years since I last wrote but it is not entirely true that I am wrapped in perfect contentment. However, it can be said much has changed for the better and it is true I have found the warmth of a beautiful heartbeat, the sanctuary of hugging cats and the melody of a dancing love since I last wrote to you.

But outside of this window, the world itself remains as confusing and conflicted as ever - technologically brilliant, emotionally fragile and morally bankrupt, surviving on credit alone. It seems with every bright corner there is a dark side. For every charitable donation, there is a bullet fired, for every innocent hope there is an unjust exploitation and for every inspirational word spoken there is a tirade of hate speech. I fear this is the world we will always know and I feel a permanent solace will never be found in such a climate.

But maybe peace is not something that is found by discovering a magical view of the world but is experienced on a temporary basis as we lurch from place to place, from people to people, from problem to solution - as we find and lose contentedness over and over. Perhaps then, rather than stop writing, my peace is in the very words that I write.

The process of writing is like blowing a balloon. Just as you release your words outwards, you are exhaling your energy into a deflated balloon and watch it grow, word by word, into a colourful airborne ornament decorating the sky. And once inflated, it is tied at one end and dispatched into the air, just as I hit the send button on this letter. One then looks upward and follows the writing rise delicately into the sky, directed by the whims of the wind and the supervision of judicious, omnipresent clouds.

The mystery and enjoyment is simply knowing the balloon could end anywhere, beyond any horizon, perhaps to be found by an inquisitive child, a curious stranger or pop inconsequentially on the brambles of a nearby thorny bush. Once it has gone from sight, it's simply time to blow another balloon, let it go and watch it go peacefully wherever fate takes it.

I have just arrived in Addis Ababa, on the slopes of the Ethiopian highlands, as it sits proudly as one of the highest capital cities in the world. Ethiopia is a country with a profound and embezzled cultural history that span millennia - the proverbial cradle of mankind, the Garden of Eden and the magical, long lost source of the Nile. However, to me, it is sadly inextricably associated with the TV campaigns of my childhood, when images of starvation and poverty in this nation would regularly cry for donations and urgent help.

Ethiopia, it seems has a remarkably similar 20th century history to that of Cambodia, a country I recently grew up in. Except for an Italian conquest during World War II, Abyssinia (and now Ethiopia) was ruled by an imperial monarch, Haile Sellasie, before being overthrown by a communist regime in the 1970s. Strife, terror and turmoil then continued until the regime collapsed in 1991 as Ethiopia stumbled into a democracy with the presence of the United Nations.

My stay here is dramatically short, nine simple days, visiting a large government hospital providing orthopaedic care to the four million inhabitants of this city. The aim is to establish a connection between the services in the world where orthopaedic care has now overcome many disabling conditions with tremendous success and those areas of the world where neglected disease still dominates. The medical world is getting smaller, hands in many countries are reaching out, almost touching one another and I believe this trip is to help just two of those hands connect, shake and maybe one day embrace fully.

I am not sure what we will discover, but I will try my best to release as many inflated balloons as possible over this ancient African landscape during my precious time here.

With love always,

Saqib

15.05.2016 – Lucy In The Roads With Pot Holes

Dearest Readers,

Today was a day to acclimatise to the environment, to allow one's lungs to breathe in the thin, dusty air whilst exploring the colourful scenes of Addis Ababa.

Our hotel is charmingly situated centrally in the city and towers high in the sparse city skyline, eleven stories tall. It seems at one time the building may have been an icon of past grandeur, with a shining glass facade, an inviting lobby adorned with cultural paintings and a now disused, but magnificent wooden radio, the size of an ice cream cart.

The hotel however seems empty, with little activity from guests and perhaps the tourists and visitors of Addis have ventured to other trendier locations. The lack of clientele has been to our benefit, as our request for the cheapest single rooms have been upgraded to large suites on the ninth floor, with wooden flooring and the luxury of a bath with shower combination. The room has all the amenities one would desire and imminently comfortable. It is by no means luxurious, with malfunctioning and dated furniture, doors and windows not quite clicking shut as they should and stark, fluorescent lighting, even in the bedside lamps.

More importantly, despite being on the 9th floor, one can hear the distinctive sounds of the city through the day and night like the room was situated in the street itself. It seems two rowdy dogs discussed local politics well into the night and in the morning, traffic rumbled heavily as soon as daylight broke, whilst a loud speaker sung Amharic anthems across the airwaves.

The lofty views from the hotel show Addis Ababa in all its vulnerable splendour. The lush green vegetation and the foothills of the Highlands can be seen for miles with a crop of new buildings sprouting amongst the sprawling corrugated tin roofs of shanty housing, each with a proud satellite dish on top.

On Sunday, the streets seemed quiet as a handful of pedestrians travelled back and forth whilst sporadic workers carried their wares or sold their goods. The roads were mostly clean and there seemed to be an order and pleasantness to the city's activities. Naturally there was a match of street football taking place as we made our way to the hospital to study our daily routine. Most businesses were closed but we took a break at a coffee shop with a remarkable similarity to Starbucks as its logo. We struggled with converting pounds to dollars to birr and I hope we get better soon!

On our routes, we were accosted by an isolated beggar or two who unfortunately seemed very persistent if not very persuasive in their request for charity. We also had a first attempt at a street mugging as a group of kids tried to grab an arm aggressively and distract me whilst another reached into a pocket. Luckily I managed to pull his hand out of my pocket before he pulled out the meagre few dollars I had taken with me on the walking trip. They scarpered quickly.

But during most of our walk, the most dangerous activity was avoiding pot holes that appeared large and deep and could easily swallow you to the depths of an unpleasant sewer.

We managed to visit Lucy, entombed in the National Museum and her final resting place. She is the skeletal remains of the oldest found hominid, living over three millennia ago in the north east of the country and a national treasure. She was named because The Beatles anthem "Lucy in the Sky with Diamonds" was playing when she was discovered. Although her cause of death is unknown, I really wonder if she met her fate by falling into one of the city's giant potholes.

Tomorrow, we remind ourselves, that as surgeons, no matter how much you study, how much you learn, how many exams you pass and how experienced your clinical practice is, we are creatures of comfort and habit. And when we are in a unique environment with unfamiliar cases and unfamiliar colleagues, we start like it was our first day of medical school, somewhat nervous and unprepared for the learning experiences to come.

With love,
Saqib

16.05.2016 - The Black Lion Orthopaedic Resistance Movement

Dearest Readers,

The black lion is a species of lion specific to Ethiopia. It is a majestic creature with a distinctive black mane covering its head and neck, worn like a warrior dressed for combat. The beautiful animal is a symbol of Ethiopia and indeed, a resistance movement against the Italian occupation in the 1930s was named after this lion. Although the organisation did not appear to have much success again the Italians, an ideological and political ethos became attached to the name which has inspired a nation. Unfortunately, the creature itself is on the verge of becoming extinct although I believe some lions still reside in a zoo in Addis Ababa.

Another Black Lion in Addis Ababa is the name of the large government hospital and the flagship centre for orthopaedic training in the country. It is here we spent our first day roaming and prowling for insight into the natural habitat of orthopaedic surgeons in the city.

There is a hive of activity around the entrances of the hospital compound, which is made up of a collection of scattered buildings, each with a different state of upkeep. A large new building is in construction in the centre of the ground whilst the orthopaedic centre, neatly tucked away in the corner comprises of a four-story building with its own wards, clinics and operating theatre complex. Like our hotel, the building has seen better days but it still has an open, spacious feel, despite its creaks and cracks. It seems to me every government hospital in every developing nation has a familiar decor of peeling paint, ceiling disrepair and overcrowded wards. But equally, every government hospital has an atmosphere of patience, resilience and hopeful staff.

The day itself was warm and long, and as we searched for the magical black lion, dressed in our camouflage of a white coat, we discovered both the expected and unexpected.

Expectedly, the patients attending the hospital presented with severe and neglected ailments. The orthopaedic pathology of poverty can be witnessed frequently across the globe and my previous expeditions have left me very familiar with identifying with the same patients here in Addis Ababa - severe infections, tumours the size of balls, high energy traumatic injuries with complications and the sequelae of difficult surgery.

Unsurprisingly also, the orthopaedic facilities are not comparable to a modern health care service with a limited inventory of supplies and equipment. Having said this, the hospital does have some advanced facilities and has access to an MRI scanner, a CT scanner, modern and plentiful computers, electronic beds and electric operating tables, a microbiology, biochemistry and pathology service as well as some respectable orthopaedic hardware. Ultimately it indicates the service being offered in the hospital are certainly better than other places across the world.

But the most surprising element of the visit was the vast number of training orthopaedic surgeons, working simultaneously and in unity within the hospital. In Ethiopia, there are only a handful of fully qualified orthopaedic surgeons scattered across the country to treat the vast population and so the orthopaedic surgeon is truly like the black lion, very low on numbers and almost extinct.

There is therefore a dire need to increase the population numbers and this hospital appears to be the breeding ground for the orthopaedic species in the country and essential for its survival. Seventy training orthopaedic surgeons cram within the department. The operating room and clinics are overflowing with these young, enthusiastic cubs. I had the opportunity to watch them work, quizzing as I went, documenting my findings and was greatly impressed with their work rate, motivation to learn, comprehensive orthopaedic knowledge, analytical thinking and technical ability. There was certainly very little to distinguish their approach and insight to surgery as compared to my colleagues in the UK, despite the vast difference in working environment, teaching programme, numbers of students and orthopaedic facilities.

Without delving into technical medical jargon and boring specifics about the training programme itself, I can say with a degree of certainty that the Black Lion Resistance Hospital is now producing an orthopaedic movement that will undoubtedly make an impact into patient care in the country, now and long into the future.

With love always,
Saqib

17.05.2016 – I Am Hungry

Dearest Readers,

Ethiopia has suffered from frequent famines over the centuries with documented droughts and food shortages every thirty to forty years. The last severe famine was in the early 1980s when a combination of a natural disaster and political turmoil led to the heart-breaking deaths of an estimated 400,000 people. Of course, this era is one we in the UK relate closely with Live Aid and Bob Geldof, pop stars singing and harrowing fundraising TV campaigns.

It has been a few days since arriving in Addis Ababa and although it is very infrequent that I have been approached on the street by an impoverished person requesting a handout, I have noticed the plea for every request has always started with the broken English phrase of "I am hungry". After hearing this very specific statement for the fourth or fifth time from different requestors, it did make me wonder whether this learnt phrase had any roots to the sad history of these terrible famines that have so regularly afflicted the nation.

Today we continued our analysis of the orthopaedic service and training programme at the Black Lion hospital. I would like to believe that throughout my writings and mumblings over many years, I have developed and displayed an honest insight into the people and environments around me with simple observations and dialogue. From my childhood, teenage years and adult life, I have genuinely loved watching the world go by and observe the manic activities of fellow travellers in this life.

In the morning, I attended and observed a teaching ward round, led by two young orthopaedic consultants and over twenty training surgeons, all dressed in their white coats as they travelled from bed to bed to review their patients. It was by far the most over-crowded ward round I had ever seen and the numbers almost doubled as a group of ten eager medical students, again in white coats crammed in to the tiny wards. I would stand quietly at the back, listen as closely as possible, whilst I waited for the expected chaos to enfold as the herd of white coats overflowed out of sight and earshot.

I tried to pay attention to both the trainers leading the round and the trainees following, whilst also simultaneously comparing the level and quality of teaching to that of orthopaedic ward-rounds that I have participated in the NHS. Furthermore, on the agenda, I wanted to review how the patients were treated and what dignity was afforded when being surrounded by a gaggle of white coated orthopaedic doctors.

The Ethiopian doctors are softly spoken, with an air of humility in their voices and with such quiet dialogue, the juniors would present their cases to the teacher that was barely audible. I wondered how it would be possible for everyone in the room to hear such a discussion but I looked around and I witnessed each trainee packed in as close as physically possible and listened in dedicated silence. There was no peripheral chatter or loss of attention for two complete hours. I only witnessed deep engagement when the teacher began questioning, probing and teaching about the case. The trainees would hurriedly make notes on what they had learnt.

I observed the teachers and their style of questioning and interaction with the students. They taught with a healthy discipline as they allowed their students time to answer, encourage right answers and explain wrong answers with firmness. When the teacher was unhappy with the level of care offered to the patient, he would reprimand the senior resident gently and ask for improvement.

The quality of the teaching being taught was relevant to the cases, appropriate to the level of any teaching I have witnessed in the UK and on some instances, beyond what I would expect.

And lastly, the patients were by and large quiet during this extensive ward round as they watched the discussions take place about their care, somewhat at the mercy of the crowd.

There were times, however, when the patients were brought into the discussion and I watched the teacher delicately examine and interact with the patient, apologising for any inconvenience or pain caused during a certain test. There was an empathy and care for the patient that was respectful to any expected bond between a doctor and his patient.

As I observed this remarkable ward round, I became acutely aware that perhaps any readers of my letters may feel my observations are exaggerated, that I view all I see with rose tinted orthopaedic eye protection and that I over emphasise positives and misread the environment I am in.

Whilst on the round, I therefore prospectively decided to jot down examples to provide some evidence for my assessment. I apologise as this may end up with details of medical jargon which I cannot avoid.

In one scenario, a debate took place about the possible complications of an amputation. The trainees answered each surgical question to an elevated level (including the principles and techniques of myodesis and myoplasty) before the debate continued onto appropriate analgesia and the absolute necessity of psychological care with the need for appropriate counselling. After the discussion, I watched as one trainee jotted down "mirror therapy for phantom limb pain" to research this concept later and it became abundantly clear they had equalled and surpassed any orthopaedic syllabus in the UK for this situation.

When the teacher explained to his trainees the need for physiotherapy and the importance of communication with the patients, he said these very words to his entire classroom:

"Even if you have explained the exercises to the patient, if the patient is not doing the exercises properly, you have not explained well enough. You must check the patient has understood what you have explained". I related very much to this as it is a teaching concept I have myself shared with my juniors.

When the teacher was unhappy with the care of the patient,

he would stress to his group to treat the patient like it was a member of their own family and would they be happy if their uncle, mother or cousin was treated in this way. This again comes out of a phrasebook I often use when I feel management could have been improved when explaining to my own juniors about caring for patients they treat.

As the ward round attended one patient who was clearly struggling with an asthmatic wheeze, the teacher discovered the patient could not afford the inhalers to alleviate his breathing problems. The teacher immediately asked all his students for a small donation and instantly everyone donated a few Ethiopian Birr and the patient managed to get his medication. This was truly a special moment to observe the care and compassion the team has for their patients.

During the ward round, I would take time to read through the patients notes so that I may assess the quality of written entries. The clerking was comprehensive, well written and beyond some entries I have witnessed in the UK notes. The writing was clear and logical with a full assessment using trauma principles, well documented diagnosis and clear management plans. The operation notes were thorough and indeed I was amazed to review a full A4 entry of a "pre-op surgical plan" that a junior doctor had written on how they would perform a biopsy procedure, detailing their plan for the position of the patient, incision and post-operative care in extreme detail. This documented forethought is almost unseen in UK orthopaedic training.

In one exchange, the teacher was unhappy the patient's notes had not been appropriately signed and he reprimanded his team, stating this is a "medicolegal issue", highlighting that Ethiopian surgeons too feel they have to be held accountable for their patient's care.

During one further questioning session with medical students, the teacher quizzed about the classification of a specific injury type (open fractures). In the modern NHS, I would not even anticipate our junior doctors to answer this question sensibly. In this exchange, the medical students also did not know the answer. However, the teacher himself humbly and openly apologised to the medical students. He softly said, "I apologise, if you do not know the answer, it is a fault with my teaching", as he led them away to teach them again.

In the afternoon, I too began teaching the junior residents in the clinic setting as I exhausted all my very recent FRCS exam knowledge rapidly on a thirsty, motivated group of doctors whose knowledge surpassed what I would expect of trainees in the UK, on a wide variety of topics. It is truly only because I have recently passed my exam that my knowledge perhaps superseded theirs by a mere amount as I taught on a wide range of clinic cases - hands, shoulder, knee, hip and spinal pathology. I began firing more questions, probing deeper into their level of understanding as I ventured into their management principles of both neglected and non-neglected pathology, including impingement syndrome of the shoulder, plantar fasciitis, trigger thumb, De Quervians tenosynovitis, SIJ examination, spino-pelvic disassociation, sacral fracture classification, osteoarthritis of the knee, the red flags of back pain and degenerate lumbar spine disease, how to read an MRI scan of the spine, the management principles of heterotopic ossification as well as the usual infected cases, tuberculosis and tumour staging of osteosarcoma (yes all these pathologies presented). They truly exhausted my knowledge as I delved deeper and deeper till I found their limit and my limit. Every patient they assessed, I found myself agreeing with their diagnosis, differential diagnosis and management plan.

As I gave more teaching points and more assignments for the trainees to read upon, I insisted they come in tomorrow to complete any questions they were unable to answer today.

One doctor smiled beamingly and said "Yes, I am excited. I will answer all your questions because you care. You care about my teaching and that is why you ask me questions. It is only for my benefit to answer".

We are often critical of the developing world, somehow feeling our styles are better and more advanced, but I feel sometimes we have a lot to learn. It is not without controversy if I was to say I truly feel medical education in the UK has lost its way as junior doctors become increasingly disengaged and disenfranchised with the profession. We have lost our mentorship, our team ethos and feeling of vocation as medical educational principles suggest "much better strategies" on how to train a surgeon. Our teams have been broken down into individual parts and been fed with sterile, tasteless meals straight from an Oxfam donation bag. It is the Ethiopian surgeons that are tasting the seasoned food of mentorship and comradeship of bedside teaching.

What I witnessed today was a traditional teaching ward round that will inspire and teach the Ethiopian surgeons of the future, the likes of which are becoming rapidly extinct today in the NHS. It would be incredibly arrogant and naive of me to suggest we teach better.

The Ethiopian surgeons are hungry for knowledge and have been famished for so long. Their training programme and knowledge acquisition is without doubt on par with my training, even if they are learning through a much different method. We also have a lot to learn in the UK and it's time we too, became hungry once more.

With love always,
Saqib

20.05.2016 – Slowly, Slowly, An Egg Will Walk

Dearest Readers,

Amharic is the official language of Ethiopia and the second most spoken Semitic language behind Arabic in the world. It is spoken by over twenty-five million people and is the working language of the Ethiopian Orthodox Church. It has its own alphabet, written from left to right and is formed up of unique characters which seem to resemble different stick men that are communicating in sign language with each other. In my brief time, I have tried to grasp a few words and phonetically get to grips with basic phrases but have not performed well, often receiving a confused look when I clear my throat and mumble some random phrase and smile goofily.

I also love reading proverbs and have always found those that emanate from Africa being extremely pleasing. Indeed, there is an old Amharic proverb, "Slowly, slowly, an egg will walk" which I have found particularly relevant to the orthopaedic services of the city and nation.

Previously, I have described a great deal of positive findings of the orthopaedic training programme and the hospital services available. In fact, if one were to read my reports thus far, it would seem Addis Ababa was at the cutting edge of orthopaedic care. However, I feel I must now balance the discussion by adding weight to the other side of the proverbial scale.

The Black Lion Hospital, like all other government hospitals in every low-income country, is overburdened with disease, not having the capacity to deal with the overflowing demand of an impoverished people. We begin in the emergency room, where patients and relatives lie on beds and on the floor, stretched out on benches and makeshift chairs, whilst awaiting much needed attention. Queues of other patients merely wait outside in the hope they soon get a place inside, literally on the shop floor.

The patients, crammed to the brim, have a wide variety of ailments as the doctors attend to them, no matter where they are lying, attaching IV drips that are held in the air by the patient's relatives. In one corner of the room, I saw an old man, sitting amongst a crowd of patients with an inappropriately sized neck collar that seemed to immobilise his entire head, it was that large. I have no doubt this was not because the doctors did not know how to size a neck collar but more likely, it was the only size available to the hospital.

In another corner, a man was lying on a bench, clearly in some sort of abdominal pain whilst another, gazed blankly upwards on an uncomfortable spinal board, likely lying there for hours if not days. Another old gentleman sat patiently with a cardboard splint around his lower leg. The cardboard was neatly folded into a triangular shape to fit the contours of his tibia and a bandage wrapped around it. It was possibly the most basic splint I have ever seen in a hospital setting.

I was told, due to the lack of ward space, sometimes patients can wait upto two to three weeks in the emergency room waiting to be admitted. The scene was absolute carnage, resembling a warzone and I would forgive anyone viewing such an environment if it induced a deep panic within.

The wards too are equally overburdened and undersupplied. Makeshift traction devices for orthopaedic limb splinting include a broomstick and bottles of water. Six patients will cram into a tiny room with barely elbow space between them let alone any privacy. The ward does however have electric beds although I could not confirm if they were working or not. The toilet facilities are certainly not the most appealing and indeed had to be closed due to a water problem during our stay.

The orthopaedic clinics are heaving with a crowded waiting room and a large consultation room that contains eight desks but only a handful of examination couches. There is only a small plaster room and wound check room, with common orthopaedic products such as synthetic fibre glass missing and specific wound dressings at a premium. Despite desperate patients with advanced pathology hobbling in and out of the clinic, the waiting list for any planned procedure is so long (over a year), their only realistic option is to hobble back to the private sector or if unaffordable, hobble home and await their fate once more.

In theatres, the image intensifier machine is broken, severely restricting the surgeons' ability to provide the best care they have learned. The installed operating lights do not work as surgeons rely on dim portable lights. The air conditioning is sadly unreliable and essential orthopaedic theatre structures such as laminar flow is missing. Demure scrub technicians appear to cope admirably with the one glove size, the only available gloves being so large it almost seems both hands could fit into just one of them. Regular problems with sterilisation of instruments and drapes can rightly delay cases although these problems are not uncommon in the NHS! Ultimately, there is just enough equipment to provide a functional service. There are good anaesthetic machines, a computer inside each operating room, a dedicated operating table and comparatively well maintained orthopaedic equipment.

Despite all these shortages and drawbacks in all areas of the hospital, it is the organisation and human resources that have been unparalleled. I still have not managed to understand how the carnage and chaos has been so expertly ordered into a meaningful and dedicated service. The patients in the emergency room were not neglected and all were being tended to. The wards were clean and orderly, with patient notes filed somehow without being lost. The clinics were in control as nurses provided a human traffic control system and in the operating theatres, the turnaround time for operations was very quick, almost like a formula one wheel change. As one wheel came off the table, the cleaning staff would scurry in, again with their oversized gloves whilst the doctors would rush to bring the next wheel in and the anaesthetists add the bolt and screws to allow the operation to start again. The pit stop timing is second to none and some may argue too fast to allow a safe transition from case to case.

And so, in conclusion, the orthopaedic facility is stretched beyond any feasible limit. However, the directors of the service are acutely aware of every impediment as they slowly find solutions to each pressing need, overcoming insurmountable hurdles over and over again.

"Slowly, slowly, an egg will walk" and it is clear here that this service is hatching into a fledgling baby bird that will one day not just walk but be able to fly.

The direst need here is not truly in orthopaedic training but in orthopaedic facilities. I am sure, with the correct infrastructure, the highly talented and trained staff would provide a truly excellent service. However, these are giant issues that need overcoming and will require significant investment from several stakeholders. This is likely only to occur parallel with socioeconomic development of the country and a health care system that can afford and maintain a world class service.

There too is a famous Chinese proverb that we quote often, "Give a man a fish and you feed him for a day. Teach a man to fish and you feed him for a lifetime" which I will now disagree with. There are plenty of orthopaedic fish that desperately need catching in Ethiopia and there are now a growing number of well-trained orthopaedic fisherman but something is still missing.

The Ethiopian orthopaedic surgeons have learnt to fish, and it may well be their fishing techniques can be refined and improved with further training and support from the outside, but without the equipment on the inside, a fisherman can yield very little fish. I would like to change the Chinese proverb to "Give a man a fish and you feed him for a day. Teach a man to fish and you feed him for a lifetime providing he has a boat, a net, and all other necessary equipment".

With love always,
Saqib

22.05.2016 – Ethiopia. "Gasp". Addis Ababa. "Gasp". Shoulder bump. "Gasp"

Dearest Readers,

My time here is almost over. I knew it was always going to be a short journey and what I have lacked in time, I have tried my hardest to make up for in sleepless energy, building relationships, communicating with all my heart and obtaining as many learning experiences as possible. My findings of orthopaedic care in the Black Lion Hospital have been confirmed over the last few days and now with more time and observation, I have had the opportunity to delve deeper, bond closer with the residents and have a better understanding of both strengths and weaknesses of the programme. Within such a small time however, it would be both foolish and naive to truly feel one has a thorough grasp of the problems facing both the surgeon and the patient as they navigate through their illnesses in Ethiopia.

The World Orthopaedic Concern has a unique opportunity here to reignite an old and beautiful relationship it has had with the Black Lion Hospital, for indeed the foundations of this incredible success were laid by forward thinking pioneers many years ago. I feel orthopaedic knowledge and care in Ethiopia is moving forward rapidly and despite its limitations, there is no doubt progress will be made quickly. As this new World Orthopaedic Concern project is forming, I feel we too must be as forward thinking as those pioneers before us and look to the future of how this great orthopaedic momentum can develop further. It begins with a relationship, a shaking of hands, and sharing a vision of both partners looking to the same horizon. I am sure our first step has been successful in this journey. This energy must now be nurtured correctly and positively for a great deal of responsibility is required to ensure outcomes are successful.

We are in a new world where volunteerism and medical

tourism is heavily scrutinised, ethical and medicolegal standards must be applied to wherever you practice and to whomever you teach. Equally, we have a burden on us, that whatever efforts we make are both productive to those receiving the effort and cost effective to those funding the programme. I am sure with the vast experience that the Wold Orthopaedic Concern has, an incredibly positive programme can commence once again.

Over the past few journal entries I have mostly described my findings of the orthopaedic programme but I have also been watching the sunrise and sunsets over this historic nation, its people, society and culture.

Injera is an East African sourdough-risen flatbread with a unique, slightly spongy texture. It is a very common form of food here and eaten frequently. Admittedly, I have truly struggled to enjoy it. The first bite always seems so pleasant and refreshing but with each bite taken, it seems to become increasingly sour to my taste buds and by the tenth bite, I can take no more. The opposite is true of my days in Ethiopia - with each passing day, the country has become sweeter and more addictive.

The country is founded on tolerance of three great religions and they all merge into the melting pot of Addis Ababa. In the morning one hears the long and rhythmic prayers of the orthodox church whilst the Muslim call to prayers intersperse throughout the day. Muslims can be seen praying in the streets, outside of their shop or in the park, whilst others make their way to church. In the hospital, patients and staff alike have no obvious reservations about each other's background. It is very reassuring to see this tolerance in a world that seems to be losing its head and heart.

The people are quiet, humble, polite and beautifully dressed. I have enjoyed the elderly Ethiopian men dress in their full three piece suits and top hats, struggle up and down the slopes of the streets of the city whilst the younger generations are equally smart, travelling to and from their work places.

Although Amharic is the national language, a good standard of English can be found in many areas of the population, which means it is easily possible to converse and make friends with local people over a coffee in a bustling or trendy cafe.

The way people greet each other is respectful and I have watched as the younger generation also enjoy a shoulder bump after each connection and I have loved it. I too have been shoulder bumping my way around the city, both with strangers and work staff that I have met along the way.

Travelling outside the city, the scenario is peaceful and breath-taking. Within two hours one is in the solace of mountains, waterfalls, lush green valleys and deep canyons as you watch a troop of Gelada monkeys play amongst themselves in their own little world by the river.

I was speaking once to an orthopaedic resident and as I was talking, I noticed he would gasp after each of my sentences. At first it struck me as odd and I even wondered if he too struggled with the thin air of this city or perhaps he struggled with asthma. But as I spoke to more and more people, I noticed this gasp was very widespread and that it was a sign that one understands what is being said. It strikes me as a beautiful way of communicating - that one would gulp in air and hold breath for a split second to demonstrate understanding, agreement and acknowledgement. I too have been practicing this gasp of agreement.

And now if you and I were to have a conversation with me about Ethiopia I will simply gasp.

Ethiopia. Gasp. Addis Ababa. Gasp. Shoulder bump! Yes! Gasp!

With love always,
Saqib

24.05.2016 – The Journey Home

Dearest Readers,

I have returned home, back from the cradle of mankind, the land of thirteen months of sunshine, the magical source of the Nile and the second most populous country in Africa.

It is becoming my tradition that my final journal entry summarises and highlights my memorable experiences, vague achievements (or lack of), and places my existence back into perspective, fitting another jigsaw piece into this manic and beautiful puzzle we all live in.

I have once again witnessed the severe orthopaedic pathology of the poor, a disease that takes its toll on a suffering people worldwide. The disease is recognisable on every continent, indiscriminate and highly predictable for where there is poverty, there is neglect and disability. I have seen patients once again grapple with the harsh realisation that their delayed treatment is fraught with difficulty, suffering is often incurable and sometimes the only salvation is to lose a body part.

I have observed the brave battle of the Black Lion Hospital, fighting hard in both treating these complex orthopaedic cases but also training a generation of future warriors to improve their chances of long term success within the country.

I have been inspired by the teachers of this programme, graduates themselves of Ethiopian orthopaedics and truly remarkable young teachers. I have been astounded by their work ethic, knowledge of orthopaedics, compassion for their patients and students, organisational skills to run the programme and effective teaching techniques. In many ways, I too wished they had been my mentors whilst I studied in the UK and without sounding ungrateful to my own teachers, the ones I have seen here are amongst the best in many ways.

I have felt both shamed and humbled by the appetite and thirst for knowledge by the young orthopaedic cubs on this Black Lion training programme. Their passion and enthusiasm to learn has far outshone mine through every stage of my career as they drained me dry of every ounce of my learning. I distributed what I had gladly, grateful that I too am perhaps at the peak of my orthopaedic knowledge mountain. I have been humbled and feel happy to have received lovely and positive feedback from many of those I interacted with.

I have managed to bond with these future surgeons in my zany way, invading their close-knit instant messaging group like a marauding colonial Italian army, but I have come in peace and not dictatorship. I have set up a friendship award programme, and a novel journal club that may allow us continued interaction, as we grow old together in the field of orthopaedics. I have promised I will stay close to these young orthopaedic lions and I hope they welcome me into their pack.

I have learnt a spattering of Amharic phrases, "Thank you, yes, no problem, be strong, how are you?" I have smiled as the Ethiopian listener laughs at my silly attempts. We have both gasped in agreement.

I have shoulder bumped my way across the city, bumping with hospital staff, visitors and strangers alike.

I have visited the remains of Lucy, the oldest known hominid known to us. I have examined her remains and wondered what orthopaedic fixation system I could use to put her bones back together again.

I have visited the church of perhaps Ethiopia oldest orthopaedic patient, a monk who lost his leg in the thirteenth century after prolonged meditation. And inside this church I have marvelled at the beautiful colours of stained glass mosaics, simple yet dazzling designs I wish I had the talent to create myself.

I have stood in a holy cave and the site of a vast number of prayers. I too have whispered a prayer for my loved ones as I have collected holy water as a gift to those that got me to the cave safely.

I have sat in front of a magical waterfall, deep in the canyons of the highlands. I have watched glorious vultures stalk the skies, swooping elegantly whilst a troop of gelada monkeys convene at the riverside, the large maned male paying special attention to one of the many females, whilst their offspring play gleefully in the water.

I have stood on a sixteenth century Portuguese bridge, with stone arches reminiscent of any medieval era or a scene from Game of Thrones. I have waved my hands happily on this bridge whilst being careful not to plunge below.

I have enjoyed the dancing and singing on a cultural evening, watching the traditional dances of the many diverse communities that make up this great nation. I have watched a dancer exhaust himself, jumping high and higher into the air, banging his drum as the crowds clap him on whilst the female dancers twirled their umbrellas.

I have walked and darted through the steep streets of Addis Ababa, photographing my way through a walking tour of historic monuments. I have experienced both kindness and petite theft simultaneously on these streets as well as meeting inquisitive strangers and well-meaning passers-by. I have been saddened by the number of beggars that I noticed more and more frequently.

I have found a healthy and deep respect for the people of this capital city, for their politeness and tolerance in many ways outshines the so called developed nations and enlightened people. I have tried to dig deeper into the plights of minority groups, issues of gender equality and individual rights of all peoples. And of course, there are significant social issues that should be debated and tackled healthily.

I have stood in awe on the foot of mountains, overlooking this vast and sprawling city from above as the sun sets beyond its horizon. And I "selfied" again from this height!

Finally, I have released seven inconsequential green, yellow and red balloons into the Ethiopian skies and watched them drift by. I have found peace by releasing them upwards, often deep into a sleepless night. For those of you who have followed this diary, I thank you for watching those haphazard balloons rise and fall peacefully with me. I am sorry, for there were many topics I have not touched upon but time was always short and my balloons had grown big enough. I was worried they may pop if they grew any larger.

I have once again returned to the warm embrace of my beloved, blessed to have found this comfort whilst we all grow older and strive to find our place, peace and role in this world.

With all my love, always.

Betam Amesiginalu (Thank you very much).
Saqib

Myanmar (2016)

Ever since leaving Cambodia in 2013, the story of Phay Samnang and the dismal outcomes of patients with bone tumours played on my mind. As I finished the research project and wrote up its disheartening conclusions many years ago, I discussed the dire need for collaboration and a cohesive healthcare service to improve care for these specific patients.

I knew that in low income countries, the treatment of bone related cancers was not on any list of priorities, for they are a rare disease, requiring multiple advanced resources and specialist expertise. Essential improvements in nutrition, clean water, primary healthcare, paediatric and maternity well-being and the treatment of infection and injury are all naturally, far more critical issues to address. Indeed, many governments and international aid organisations are striving to improve care in these sectors. However, this did not mean those unfortunate patients with rare and difficult conditions should be neglected and it did not feel easy for me to ignore or forget the story of Phay Samnang and the other patients in the study. I wanted the research and our travels around the villages of Cambodia to lead to an improvement in global care for those people to be so unfortunately affected, where modern treatment was unavailable.

As I returned home from work one day, I contemplated the enormity of the problem, knowing if I was to start such project, it would likely take decades of perseverance and strife to make a meaningful and palpable difference. However, I realised I was coming to the end of my surgical training and that I still had decades ahead of me as well as the desire to make a start. I have realised, from all my travels, that often it just takes an initial push and hopeful energy to make a long-lasting difference.

And so via an acquaintance from the organisation World Child Cancer, I contacted an oncologist in Yangon, Myanmar, whom I heard was dynamic, passionate and exceptionally motivated.

I wrote briefly as a stranger, explaining my passion for patients with bone cancers, my research in Cambodia and whether I could learn about the experiences and difficulties being faced in Myanmar with similar patients. I was not really expecting a reply or indeed a positive one, but within a few days, I received an e-mail expressing interest in the project and within a month, I had a formal letter of invitation. Therefore, based on a few short emails, I flew out to Yangon, very much in unchartered territory, for I was not affiliated with any established project. I was just a random doctor, in search of knowledge and collaboration, in hope to kick start a potentially decade long project into life. I truly did not know what to expect, and in many ways, unsure in which direction I would end up travelling.

26.11.2016 – Every Raindrop, Puddle, River, Waterfall

Dearest Readers,

Every raindrop starts with a burst from a restless cloud and falls to the ground from a seemingly generous sky. Thereafter, it seeps into the depths of the soil or connects directly to a waterway, meandering through the middle of a scenic journey of variable length before concluding to a final location, evaporating crisply into the air and ready to burst from the skies once more.

International medical aid is somewhat like this flow of water, falling from the sky and then running in various forms, depths and movements. I always felt, should I ever pursue international work into the latter aspects of my life, I would enlist in a large organisation and contribute within the mainstream river of their work. And yet, so far, I have mostly worked within thriving smaller organisations, just little streams and tributaries that contribute energetically to the overall flow of aid but through very specific parts of the world.

Previously I wondered why there was even a need for these small charities when the global organisations seemed so much more robust, more effective, better funded and more powerful. Their TV, newspaper and radio adverts surely promised that a donation to their organisation was the only solution to solve all the needs of all the people in all the places of the world. It truly seemed futile that smaller charities would have anything meaningful to contribute that a global organisation could not perform.

However in reality, all diverse types of water flow are required, for the streams of smaller organisations may well be able to connect quicker and traverse the rocky lands and higher ground that a large swathe of water could not access. Indeed, all organisations, like water, in their various forms and directions are ultimately needed to work harmoniously together if global improvement in care is to be maximally achieved.

But sometimes the water flow of international aid-work is not always efficient and it can be wasteful or worse still, harmful. Water can become stagnant, in murky puddles or boggy swamps whilst other waterworks seem not to connect, serve limited purpose or even run in counter currents to others. Some aid-work is in deep isolation, a giant lake with no links whilst others crash into each other like waves to assert dominance and compete for power. Furthermore, some parts of the world receive excessive rainfall whilst others areas are still suffering from major droughts. And even more worryingly, sometimes poorly distributed aid can overwhelm and flood the land that it seeks to assist. The results of this unpredictable and haphazard nature of aid make the map somewhat difficult to navigate and know where one should swim safely and most effectively. Should you sail on the calmness of a static lake? Or make a splash in a smaller puddle? Or drift downstream in the river? For surely each option has great purpose, rewards and pitfalls.

My previous journeys have always been with a clear role in a smaller organisation, with an objective and a specific mandate. I arrive today in Yangon, Myanmar in somewhat unique circumstances for it is the first time I am venturing out on my own, with no institution or non-governmental organisation to truly be a part of.

This time, I have no instruction. The project I envisage does not yet exist for along my travels I have identified a neglected need for a small group of patients I feel passionate about but they appear to be suffering from a drought. For this reason, perhaps I now need to fall from the sky like a single raindrop, not knowing where I will land or where I will flow. It seems the hardest and most unpredictable place to start any journey.

But I promised myself once I completed my higher surgical training I would dedicate a portion of my life towards international aid and maybe if I evaporate myself, this tiny raindrop can burst from the cloud, develop into a little stream of energy that distributes a semblance of aid to those specifically I have seen in the world who are going without.

Right now, I have arrived in Yangon, Myanmar, but truly I do not know where I have landed but I will find out shortly. I will update more about the project concept in due course.

With love always,
Saqib

27.11.2016 – The Railway Journey Of Bone Tumours

In the developing world, with a limited infrastructure, there are many essential priorities in order to improve the health of the nation. Similar to a transport system, healthcare systems also require different levels of well connected, functioning parts around the country to treat patients well.

Access to clean water, shelter, reliable food sources are the immediate priorities followed by maternal and paediatric care, vaccinations and primary medical facilities. Next come life-saving medications and access to basic investigations and emergency treatments, all whilst other important public health measures are implemented such as transport management, occupational safety legislation and medical regulations.

As these become established and improve, secondary and tertiary healthcare systems are required, where more advanced treatment and specialist care can be provided - safe surgery, inpatient medical care and robust diagnostic facilities for example. Beyond this, there is also the crucial importance of other allied specialities including physiotherapy, orthotics, social support amongst others. Each one of these aspects of care become an important station on a health care railroad to successfully treating as many patients as possible, for as many conditions as possible.

Currently in many low-income countries, sadly there is still a large proportion of impoverished people who lack reliable primary care facilities let alone the advanced railways that are required to treat the more complex conditions of the human body. Unfortunately, bone tumours are one of those complex conditions that are incredibly difficult to treat in such circumstances.

A primary bone tumour is a rare but incredibly sad disease, for it often presents in late adolescence, when we, as humans are most alive, when we truly begin to love, to dream, to have hope, to develop ideals that we strive to live by. The tumour presents as a slow growing swelling in relation to the bone, with variable amount of pain as it begins to invade the surrounding area and soon spreads elsewhere to the body. In the most modern healthcare settings, with all available treatment options, even after early detection, the prognosis is still quoted at best, 70-80% survival at five years for some tumours.

Bone tumours therefore still represent significant challenges to even the most advanced medical transport system, let alone the developing world, where any failings in this complex network of health care ultimately results in a grim ending.

If a patient does not have access to reliable primary care, they will often present when the tumour is too advanced. Even if the patient presents early, there may not be the correct diagnostic facilities to make an accurate diagnosis. Even if a correct diagnosis is made, there may not be the access to limb saving surgery or chemotherapy. Even if there is access, the patient or their family may not be able to afford the ticket for fear of crippling debt. And even if they can afford it, there lies the vast social stigma of the amputation, chemotherapy side effects and limited disability provisions. And if the patient is lucky enough to have overcome all those obstacles and embarks on this daunting journey, the chances of survival at best are still only four in five.

But if their tumour cannot be treated, if any of those railways fail, there is the awful prospect of a severely painful tumour, or respiratory complications taking over, with no real palliative care and a sad demise.

I still remember travelling through the villages of Cambodia, with photographs of patients who once had osteosarcoma many years ago, in the hope of finding them or at least their outcomes. And as expected, the results we found were miserable, with only eight percent surviving. Although the findings were predictable, I never forgot the plight of these patients, the challenges they faced in their young lives, and the improvements that were needed to give future patients a fighting chance.

And so I am beginning the Bone Cancer Network, a conceptual railroad, to bring patients, clinicians, facilities, funders and locomotive energy together, no matter where they are in the world, no matter the healthcare system. It is true that the treatment of bone tumours tests a nations healthcare system to the limit in every facet, but challenges are there to be overcome, and the more I have seen of inspiring leaders of healthcare in various under resourced settings, and the daily improvements being made, I am sure that we can achieve a better railway, with faster trains, all running as smoothly as possible, no matter where we are born.

With love,
Saqib

29.11.2016 – A Collection Of Drawings: Where There Is Life There Is Hope, Where There Is Love There Is Life.

Dearest Readers,

When I arrived in Yangon, I knew little of what to expect. I knew Myanmar had a complex and rich history, steeped in Buddhist tradition but blighted by colonial occupation and wars throughout the nineteenth and twentieth century. I knew Yangon was its largest city, a population of over five million people and I knew it's most historic landmark was the Schwedagon Pagoda, a shimmering golden monument that towers into the skyline, where relics of four previous Buddhas are enshrined. But beyond this, my knowledge of the city, the country, its people were completely unknown.

Today I visited the Yangon Children Hospital, with little more than a few email communications explaining my passion for those patients suffering with bone tumours throughout the developing world. The Children's Hospital is a large, 1300 bedded governmental hospital, established in the 1960s and continues to thrive to this day, with a combination of government and international aid support.

The hospital is busy, providing care to some of the poorest patients in the country and I wondered what little time the departments would have for a random visitor from the UK knocking on their door. I am all too aware of the flood of good intentioned charities and non-governmental work that can actually hinder progress, waste valuable clinical time and energy of the staff or over burden a perfectly functioning hospital. However, what followed was nothing short of humbling and inspirational.

The oncology department had organised a round table meeting, between themselves, the internal orthopaedic department and external adult orthopaedic surgeons from the general hospital, specifically to discuss the difficult condition, burdens and challenges of bone tumours. I somehow felt my simple visit was the spark to bring this worldwide problem to a local meeting between very motivated and articulate staff. Amazingly, a full lunch was provided for all the attendees, a treat that is rare to find in most hospital meetings in the UK these days. The junior doctors presented their cases of bone tumours whilst the patients were specifically bought into the meeting to discuss their care. The pathway and the hardships of the patient was described, the facilities available and investigations discussed, the outcomes debated.

One patient was a nine-year-old who had presented in the very advanced stages of her cancer, where little could be offered, the familiar tale of what I expected to find, as she lost her battle soon after.

But then another case was presented, a slight eight-year-old girl, who hopped into the room on crutches along with her beaming father. She had been treated with all the correct chemotherapy, both before and after her leg amputation, and two years on, still remains disease free.

The family had to relocate to the city for her treatment, practically spending twelve months living in the hospital as their daughter underwent the throws of chemotherapy, her father giving up his job as a rice seller, slowly going into an unpayable debt. Even though the treatment was free, the associated costs of giving up one's livelihood, transport and social costs over such a long period of time were devastating.

And yet he smiled proudly, so grateful for the care his daughter had received, so happy his daughter was still with him to this day. He delightfully pulled out all her drawings she had made whilst in hospital which he had remarkably kept so neat and tidy, stored away under her hospital bed, in a preciously protected little bag. One by one, colourful pictures of dresses came out, different designs, carefully drawn by the little girl, as she wanted to be a fashion designer one day. Indeed, so motivating and supportive was the little girl's family, they even commissioned one of her drawings to be made into a real dress, a bright pink piece with a multitude of ribbons adorning the sleeves.

And in that one drawing truly lies the message of this disease and this little project, for adversity can be overcome, if the chances are available, if the cogs of the machine work together, if all happens to go well. For where there is life, there is hope. And where there is love, there is life. And whilst there are still colourful drawings being drawn by happy children when fate had suggested otherwise, there are still reasons to be happy in this world.

With love always,
Saqib

01.12.2016 – Big Brother, Little Brother

Dearest Readers,

Yangon is a fascinating city, located in the lower aspect of mainland Myanmar. It was once the proud capital of its nation, before it relinquished the role to Naypyitaw in 2006. I have been here for only a few days now, but much of the city brings back memories of my time in Phnom Penh, another bustling city in the heart of Southeast Asia.

Indeed, the similarities are so familiar to me, it feels like the two cities are genetically related, like long lost brothers. Geographically, they both are situated on the confluence of two rivers, Yangon at the meeting place of the Yangon and Bago rivers as they make their way to the Andaman Sea. Phnom Penh, also in the southern aspect of Cambodia, unites the Tonle Sap and Mekong rivers as they converge towards Vietnam and exit into the South China Sea.

Both cities have an extensive colonial past, Yangon being a part of the British Empire, whilst Phnom Penh fell under the rule of French Indochina. As a result, colonial architecture is littered throughout the older neighbourhoods of both cities, so much so that Phnom Penh, in its colonial opulence was titled the "Paris of Asia", whilst Yangon was known as the "Garden City of the East".

Both populations live bustling, animated lives, as the people plough through their labour during the sweltering heat and work well into the night, whilst the city lights switch on with the activities of evening markets, food stalls and social events.

And the people of both cities seem all so lovely with a humble, polite affection that is warming and charming to be around. Yangon, like Phnom Penh is a cosmopolitan, tolerant melting pot of indigenous dwellers, generations of migrating families from all across the Asian continent, and newer migrants, often from Western countries seeking new employment in this developing Asian climate. Lastly, tourists dot around from place to place, looking for adventure and enlightenment through their travels.

And in tourism, further parallels lie, as it can be argued neither Yangon or Phnom Penh in their own rights have immense tourist appeal, but both locations are a hub and gateway to the tourist jewels of their countries, Angkor Wat in Cambodia, an ancient, magnificent temple city and Bagan in Myanmar, a spiritual landscape with hundreds of towering golden pagodas on the background of jaw dropping scenery.

But with the genetic similarities between these two cities, also come their differences, and it felt to me, in this family, Yangon was the older brother and Phnom Penh the cheeky younger sibling.

Yangon seemed more rigid, structured and disciplined, like it had a great responsibility weighing on its shoulders. It is an incredibly safe city, perhaps with the least crime in the entire region, for it has no time even for petit offences. Motorbikes are banned on all roads, ensuring only a cascade of endless cars smog up the air in gridlock traffic. Its riverside is more industrial, commercial, and business-like without any true scenic pleasure but inland there are pretty lakes in order to escape the fog of smoke and dust.

The nightlife in the city is restrained and there is a respectful lack of flirtatious and vulgar activities that are so prominent in some other South East Asian cities. Overall, the facade of Yangon seemed more withered, with peeling paints and crumbling walls of the old colonial buildings, and even the recently built apartments looking somewhat downbeat and decayed. But the city is handsome, in its sharp, solid, stern outlook.

Phnom Penh on the other hand has a more juvenile vibrancy. Motorbikes will scoot in and out of the traffic lanes, with any number of people or highly stacked merchandise as passengers balancing on the back. Tuk tuk drivers will rest in the back of their carts, their bellies happily exposed, resting in the midday sun as they call out joyfully to potential customers. Along the riverside, groups of people will be gathering for communal exercises or to play games of hackie-sack, whilst tourist-boats float on by.

Music will be blurting out throughout many venues well into the night, as locals and tourists express their karaoke talents and there are the more notorious, seedier parts of the city, where there is likely unhappiness and exploitation behind the colourful, dazzling lights.

These two brothers, big Yangon and little Phnom Penh reminded me of the orthopaedic family as today I met a number of incredibly friendly and motivated surgeons at the Yangon Orthopaedic Hospital. From Professors to junior consultants, all had prepared presentations and gave up their time to discuss the difficulties of bone cancers in the region. Indeed, their experience and expertise vastly outweighed mine as clearly their department receives a huge amount of bone tumours from the population. The conversation was open and enlightening as each consultant passionately showed me their cases on their ward, detailing every problem. I learned great amounts about the available and missing facilities, as well as the difficult pathways facing patients in Myanmar with bone cancers. It was a highly successful introduction to bone cancer management in Myanmar and at the end of the meeting, I was flabbergasted to be presented with a gift from the surgeons whilst also being invited to an evening meal out with them all. Once again, similar to the visit at the Children's Hospital, I was incredibly humbled, on the background of a few brief email enquiries, to have had so much energy and attention focused on this bone cancer problem, from a clearly very busy department.

But aside from learning about bone cancer management here, more importantly, I connected once more with hugely impressive surgeons in the world, dedicated, knowledgeable and experienced, who lovingly seek partnerships, sharing of knowledge and improvement of their facilities, all for the betterment of their patients. Indeed, it seems to me, the current model of teaching and training that occurs in medical aid work, is all too parental, the concept of teaching others "how to do it right". In fact, I believe teaching and training in the developing world should be much more like a brotherhood. I feel there is a lot more we can learn from each other's experiences then dictate mantra that may or may not be applicable to all medical cultures and scenarios.

Sometimes we must be the responsible big brother, but sometimes must be prepared to be joyful little brother, learning from our experienced relatives in this highly connected and amazing world.

With love always,
Saqib

03.12.2016 – The Richest Man In The World

Dearest Readers,

As a boy, I would wander into the late evenings with my four legged friend, searching for adventures and meanings of the long lost mysteries that make the world spin. I would dream of being a superstar footballer or a songwriter, expressing cryptic, love filled lyrics to millions of fans. I dreamt of being a war journalist, wearing a tin pot hat, avoiding bullets whilst describing international crises that were occurring around me. And at the end of my journey, I planned to disappear into the solitude of the mountain tops, where I could retire from the drum beats of the human escapade and find some solace.

But as I continued my long walks, and those dreams became less readily plausible, I became more focused on only seeking answers that I could discover and not ponder on solutions to never-ending problems that were beyond me to solve. I realised the more I actually wanted in life, the more I forgot what I already had. But the more I valued what I truly already had, the less I craved or needed.

And now, as I grow older, each day it seems I want less, and each day, I have steadily become richer. As I return back from Myanmar, for the first time in my life, I truly feel like the richest man in the world - for there is nothing that I desire that I do not already have.

My wardrobe is beaten up, old and out of fashion, but the clothes hang loosely on my shoulders, warm my spirit and are easy, to maintain. I am comfortable in my skin, and how the world perceives me, no matter my comical look.

My trusted four-year-old phone does all the communicating I need, quickly and efficiently, despite its weary cracks and occasional malfunction. My clinky clunky laptop, so behind in its technology and speed, still allows me to pour my creative soul into all of my projects.

My car, drives me lovingly from place to place, without much fuss or fault, playing the radio songs as we ride together around the city.

My home, although creaky, provides a comfortable bed, and an ambience in which I am relaxed, settled and cosy.

My orthopaedic education has recently attained a level where my inner confidence and outer standard allows me to think freely, respect myself and others around me. Despite still having so much to learn, a peace of mind has allowed me to rest whilst I still grow.

My well-being is good, with all my parts still moving and functioning and inner organs appearing to do what the instruction manual said they should.

My family, loving and healthy, are my greatest role models and remain supreme sources of guidance, inspiration and motivation.

My beautiful wife, loving and humble, cherishes all that I am, whether I deserve it or not. She tolerates my faults, and accepts my eccentricities, standing with me, happily producing terrible selfies together all over the world.

My memories, my greatest treasure, vivid and rich, allow me to sleep well and focus on creating more memories for the future treasure chest.

I have truly found my peace with God and all the creations and peoples of the world, for I have my solace, knowing my time here is finite, my impact on others finite, my achievements finite, my dreams finite, my wealth finite, my life finite - and should it end tomorrow or in another fifty years, I am happy to know I have lived, loved and given it all, with all I had, with the riches I was given - for I truly am the richest man in the world.

It is now time to distribute this inner wealth, the best way I know how with kindness and generosity, hopefully beginning with this new project, the Bone Cancer Network - for there are those in the world far less fortunate than I am.

With love always,
Saqib

Haiti (2017)

Ever since leaving Haiti, I stayed in close communication with the founders of the Haiti Hospital Appeal, now renamed and established as Hope, Health, Action. I watched them as their project grew from the rubble of the earthquake to a thriving rehabilitation unit as well as now providing paediatric and maternity care. I cheered them on in total awe as they successfully supported a paraplegic patient from Haiti to compete in the London 2012 Paralympic Games.

I always promised I would return to their project, should they ever feel they needed any skills I could offer, once I had finished my training. And so, it was perfect timing, when I was invited out to Haiti to celebrate the ten-year anniversary of the opening of the first clinic, coinciding with a period of annual leave I had just booked, almost a year after I had completed my final FRCS exams.

I was told the hospital was now treating orthopaedic patients and surgical facilities were available. I naturally had an infinite number of questions about the service they were providing and in which areas they needed my assistance for improvement.

"Why don't you come and see, evaluate our service, advise us?", Carwyn asked.

In January 2017, I flew out with my old friend, this time via Miami, to see what difference seven years of arduous work could make.

22.01.2017 – From Where We Came

Dearest Readers,

There is a beautiful phrase in Arabic which is said in the saddest times, upon the passing of a fellow human being. It translates simply into English as "from Him we came and unto Him we must return." It truly represents the simplicity of our journey, a clear beginning and end, indisputable that we all too, will return from wherever or to whomever we came.

But sometimes we also return to the past, to different points in our lives on our individual timelines, from where we came in our own history, those very defining moments that nurtured and developed us. This year promises to be a year of return for me, for I have scheduled trips to Cambodia, Pakistan and Haiti, all destinations that have influenced me greatly in unique and profound ways.

I am currently on the flight to Cap-Haitien, the second city of Haiti. It is an area I visited in 2010, a month after the earthquake that destroyed so many lives. Although I did not witness the first hand devastation of the earthquake itself, I certainly was exposed to the severe medical and social consequences of the disaster. Furthermore, it was with deep sadness that I witnessed the instant fragility of life, present on site at a landslide where a school collapsed, resulting in the departure of four children from this world.

However, I also witnessed an infinite love and compassion of fellow humans, coming together in their masses to the aid of those that desperately needed it. Those acts of kindness, donating time, energy and love have always stayed with me as a constant reminder that the human psyche, when united and compassionate, can achieve beautiful and wondrous achievements.

I left an organisation now known as Hope, Health, Action with the utmost belief that they had the talent, energy and determined loyalty to improve the long-term lives of those impoverished in Haiti. And indeed, since the earthquake, their achievements have been nothing short of miraculous. They have gone on to develop a thriving spinal injuries rehabilitation unit, as well as a fully functioning maternity and paediatric centre - all self-sustaining whilst empowering the local population.

As I left Haiti in 2010, I promised the founder of the organisation, that I too would return to Haiti, once I was better educated, more experienced, and if my skills would be useful for their long-term vision. I always stayed in touch, watching and admiring from a distance as this organisation blossomed, truly succeeding beyond all expectations. And after all these years it so happened, that as I completed my final exams and inched nearer to the end of my orthopaedic surgical training, the organisation is also looking to expand their services into this field of trauma and orthopaedics, with groundwork and facilities potentially amenable for such a project. This trip also happens to coincide with the ten-year anniversary of the opening of the first clinic building in the hospital, and so there will be much scheduled events and celebrations during this stay!

In sincerest honesty, I did not truly believe that when I left in 2010, I would actually be returning in any capacity. Yet it has become a promised and humble return to where I came seven years ago, where I learnt so much and where I hope I will once again, learn so much more. It is only a short trip, but sometimes it's those short, fleeting moments that stay with you for a lifetime.

With love always,
Saqib

26.01.2017 – Beyond Mountains There Are Mountains

Dearest Readers,

When I first visited Haiti in 2010, I entered by land, on a rickety tickety bus. Although the scenery was intriguing - lush greenery riddled with litter strewn slums in the foreground, whilst in the background were empowering hills and distant mountains, I was not able to fully appreciate the majestic land that is Haiti. On this occasion, flying into Cap-Haitien, it was possible to take in the full scale of the dramatic Haitian landscape. As we began our descent, one could appreciate an endless land mass of towering, rugged hills of incredible glory, surrounded by the crystal blue Caribbean waters.

Along with those stunning and breath-taking scenes, Haiti also has an incredible history of strife that will equally catch your breath. Like all colonised nations, there is a history of occupation, disempowerment, brutality, rebellion, counter rebellion, foreign meddling and ultimately misery. The history of Haiti is one that is particularly unpleasant to read, and ever since Columbus landed on this island during his first voyage of discovery, Haiti seems to have lurched from one calamity to the next.

Initially Spanish and then French occupation consumed the first few centuries since European invasion, eventually eliminating the local indigenous population. The country, under French rule became notorious for the worst condition of slaves in the region, many slaves dying in brutal circumstances and women choosing to abort their children rather then bring life into misery.

A slave rebellion led to independence in 1804 and has been the only recorded slave rebellion to achieve such success. However, the country was never able to prosper and an equally violent American invasion and occupation from 1915-1934, aimed at establishing American foreign influence in the region, led to the deaths of many thousands of innocent people.

Tragedy has also struck in the form of natural disasters. Hurricanes and typhoons have regularly lashed through the country with carefree abandon, destroying any semblance of infrastructure along the way. More recently, of course there was the devastating earthquake in 2010 maiming the entire country along with another very destructive typhoon in 2016 and a cholera outbreak, also in 2010.

Since returning to Haiti, I have learnt a beautiful new proverb, "Beyond mountains, there are more mountains". Although there are many interpretations, the concept of a huge challenge after huge challenge seems to fit well with both Haiti's rugged terrain and its heart-breaking history, as well as the never-ending natural tragedies, affecting the impoverished people.

But mountains are also being climbed, and the hospital I am visiting too has been successfully climbing mountains for many years. Since 2007, starting off with a small clinic aimed at improving maternity care and a centre for disabled children, the hospital has miraculously developed a spinal rehabilitation unit, after responding to the earthquake and the needs of patients paralysed by the rubble. Now after ten years of climbing this mountain, the hospital runs a maternity centre, delivering one-hundred-and-fifty babies per month, including the ability to perform Caesarean sections. Children have access to medical care, and a new emergency room and surgical department have recently been built.

But beyond this ten year climb are more mountains, for there are further challenges, further peaks in the horizon that must be climbed. The hospital is now keen on developing a trauma service, to cater for the numerous injuries being sustained, leaving women, men and children permanently disabled. In Haiti, motorcycle crashes occur by the bus load, work place accidents are commonplace, children fall regularly from tall trees, and violence still leaves fellow humans badly hurt. The ability to manage trauma injuries in Haiti is complex and baffling, and climbing this new mountain almost seems impossible, like an Everest of all problems and mountains combined. But beyond mountains there are mountains, and I am sure this trauma mountain can and will be climbed, slowly, surely, painfully and with great purpose, to one day gaze upon the next majestic, beautiful, mountain ready to be conquered in Haiti.

With love always,
Saqib

28.01.2017– The Rubik's Cube Of Trauma

Dearest Readers,

I am staying in a little enclave constructed specifically for hospital volunteers, lovingly known as "The Village". In comparison to the accommodation seven years ago, I am living in relative luxury.

The Village is a walled and gated plot of land with a few single storey buildings connected with a concrete path, surrounded by a collection of wandering, jolly animals and colourful agricultural activity. The buildings are small dormitories, filled with single beds and bunkbeds, designed to accommodate up to four volunteers in each room. Each little block of rooms has a shared toilet and shower facility.

There is a large common room, with an eclectic mix of comfortable seating options and a variety of tables to eat at, with a smaller kitchen on the side. Outside is a wooden deck, covered from the sun by a leafy pergola, within which a dove happily nests its offspring.

The Village is an upgrade in amenities from my last visit. Electricity is more consistent, powered reliably by the sun rather than Haitian infrastructure. Food, although basic, is very nutritious and is cooked by Haitian workers, tenderly and lovingly prepared each morning and evening. Filtered water is readily accessible and there is ample space to not feel claustrophobic should you ever need room to breathe.

However, some creature comforts are still lacking, cold showers result in a tingling and jolting start to the day and a lack of connectivity leaves the bare minimum of Internet access - enough bandwidth to send an intermittent and sporadic not-so-instant message to loved ones. Of course, there are still the insects, mosquitoes and dare I say, very large crawling creatures.

But the Village is an enormously peaceful place. Chickens and hens click and cluck through the gardens and three wonderful dogs greet you upon arrival, wagging their tails in salutation. A peacock roams the grounds, waiting for the opportune moment to display its array of green and blue feathers to any admiring onlookers. The days are hot but the evenings are cool, as a variety of music genres either soothes or blurts out from a Bluetooth speaker. The nights are calm, star studded and perfect for marshmallow toasting by a low burning bonfire.

There is an upbeat and vibrant feeling throughout the day amongst the volunteers - as always, courteous, caring, respectful and sometimes hilariously comical. With the lack of outside communication and access to the internet, evenings are filled with immersive conversation, sharing of stories and feelings, or bonding over random board games.

However, amongst all this activity and visual stimulation, it was a solitary Rubik's cube that drew my biggest attention - for this little game, sitting in the middle of the common room, paralleled so much of the project I have come to witness.

The Rubik's cube is a complex puzzle, multi-coloured, addictively enticing and a game I have never ever come to understand or make progress with. Its objective is to match all six sides of the cube with the same colour of nine smaller squares by making multiple twisting and turning motions on the face of the cube. And despite my general incompetence of the puzzle, I have never stopped trying to figure it out.

The Rubik's cube summarises the trauma puzzle in Haiti, and within the hospital, for providing high quality care to the multiply injured patient is incredibly complex. Like the Rubik's cube, the puzzle is multifaceted and requires multiple components all working together, all squares well aligned and organised. Yet in such an impoverished setting, trauma care is as boggling as the cube itself - the squares all jumbled up in a mix and match configuration. It truly is hard to know which face to turn first and in which direction to have any obvious way of solving the challenge.

In our fleeting time in Haiti, we have already witnessed the trauma one would expect in this setting - severe and disabling injuries as a result of high speed road traffic accidents, where safety is a non-existent concern. We have seen men badly injured due to the violence of other men, and children playing in unsafe environments. The frequency and severity of high energy trauma is very much akin to that I witnessed in South Africa many years ago and I have no doubt each day and night many lives are being destroyed by accidents where safety and optimal care cannot be found.

Yet the ability to treat injuries is somewhat difficult here, for the sides of the Trauma Rubik's cube are not fully solved. The infrastructure of the hospital is only just being established and a reliable supply chain of consumable items for safe surgery have not been found - the hospital, like many others in the austere environment, relying on sporadic and uncertain donations. Processes such as clear patient pathways, from the corner of a roadside accident to the centre of the operating room have not been fully defined and allied services such as a blood bank or microbiology and pathology services are not readily available anywhere in the northern territories of the country.

This boggling dilemma is very much like the Rubik's cube sitting in the common room. I know the cube is there, taunting me, waiting to be solved and it's impossible not to impulsively pick up the cube and turn some dials, make some rotations to make some progress. One sometimes feels the cube cannot be solved, but from my brief visit here, it is abundantly clear that two squares on this trauma cube are permanently here to stay. Firstly, trauma in this land is debilitating at an incredibly high frequency and secondly, the will, courage and determination of the hospital to tackle this problem is undeniable and uncountable. It is these two squares that are already aligned on this puzzle and now we must simply work to solve the rest, one turn at a time.

With love always,
Saqib

30.01.2017 - The Surgical Tourist

Dearest Readers,

It is time to leave Haiti for the second time. This will be my last diary entry on this journey for it truly has been the shortest stay. I feel again somewhat like a tourist as I have travelled many miles from home, visited amazing places, witnessed phenomenal achievements by great people, made inspiring new friends, taken comedy selfies and am now packing my bags to return back to a life of security and comfort.

I have always felt in the field of developing medical services and treating patients in an austere environment, it requires a lifetime of dedication in one small corner of the world to make a meaningful impact. It would take years upon years of overcoming obstacles to gradually help empower a deserving population who lack access to even the most basic care. And yet on my short and simple travels from 2008 onwards, I have often felt like a healthcare tourist, for I only come, I only see, I only write my letters but I never truly conquer and achieve. I do know, however, as I head closer toward the apex of my surgical training, I may be soon ready to climb my own mountain.

During the stay we have witnessed a ten-year anniversary of a project that truly dared to conquer, by staying in one place, by being committed to one cause, by never giving up despite the hardships and adversities. Many volunteers have travelled back and forth, month after month and year upon year, assisting a local community that had no option of travelling away but remain focussed on their humble targets of improving their own circumstances. Indeed, after talking to many volunteers involved with this project, it seems my seven year absence was the longest absence of anybody who has returned to see the work that has taken place, for everyone else returned sooner and on such a regular basis. To that end,

I still shoulder some guilt whilst simultaneously relieved to fulfil my promise to return and offer what little I can again.

When I last left Haiti, I talked of the heroes I had met, and the union of all humanity collaborating in times of extreme human distress. But it is the heroes that stayed longer, that sacrificed more and prolonged their donation that have remained the unsung heroes ever since the world has re-forgotten about Haiti.

The biggest lesson I have learnt, as I fly around the world, still as a surgical tourist, is a re-affirmation that to achieve anything substantial, it requires a lifetime of dedication, of never giving up hope, persevering despite the craziness that surrounds us, by maintaining a positive, hopeful outlook, and by taking as many zany selfies along the way.

Now after years of surgical tourism and completing surgical training within the UK, I will continue a journey of life-long learning for the betterment of my future patients. I plan to embark on a series of international fellowships to further enhance my surgical skills before utilising all I have gained to improve surgical care in impoverished locations.

I end this final letter, with a promise to strive to be the very best I can be and for as long as I can be. It is time to finally stop writing, knowing that I have found my peace in the world. Now, I must simply find my place within it.

With love always,
Saqib

Selected photographs (2008-2017)

At the Drakensberg Mountains, 2008

Bunjee jump at the Victoria Falls, 2009

Microflite over the Victoria Falls, 2009

Game walk with lion, 2009

Mtunzini beach, 2008

Making friends in South Africa, 2009

Ngwelezana Hospital football team, 2009

The Haiti Hospital Appeal "Spinal Unit", 2010

Valentine's Day Celebrations on the wards, HHA, 2010

At the scene of the school collapse, Haiti, 2010

Visit from the US Marines, Haiti, 2010

Vital aid of Pop Tarts, Haiti, 2010

Tented hospital, earthquake relief, Haiti, 2010

Photograph by Christine Finn, journalist

Tented hospital, earthquake relief, Haiti, 2010

Photograph by Christine Finn, journalist

A funeral in Haiti, 2010

Pakistani floods, 2010

Destroyed roads, Pakistan, 2010

Tented displaced camps, Pakistan, 2010

Cheeky children, displaced camps, Pakistan, 2010

The road is a river, Pakistan, 2010

The waters are rising, Pakistan, 2010

Inside of flooded health care unit, Pakistan, 2010

After initial clean of health care unit, Pakistan, 2010

Indy's boots, Pakistan, 2010

Sharing food at sunset with the Turkish volunteers, Pakistan, 2010

The hotel room make-shift store room, Pakistan, 2010

Sim BHU computer game, making progress, locked drugs cabinet, Pakistan, 2010

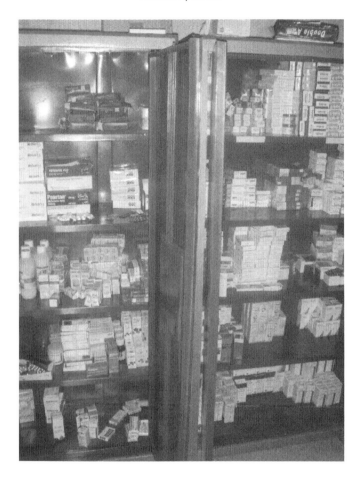

Sim BHU computer game, making progress, clean linen and treatment room, Pakistan, 2010

Sim BHU computer game, making progress, happy game player,
Pakistan, 2010

Heroes and goodbyes, the Turkish team leaves Pakistan, 2010

The Ministry of Corruption, eventually receiving donations at
nightfall, Pakistan, 2010

The AJW book project, AJW's destroyed book collection, Pakistan, 2010

AJW receiving signed book from all volunteers, Pakistan, 2010

AJW and I outside the clinic, Pakistan, 2010

In tribute to my grandparents, Pakistan, 2010

In tribute to my grandparents, Pakistan, 2010

Surgery on the shoulder of giants, Cambodia, 2013

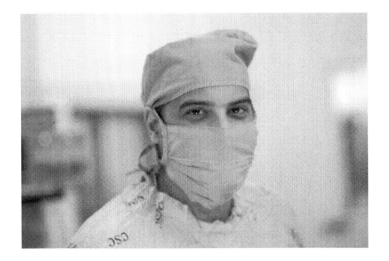

The temples of Cambodia, 2013

The United Nations of Medicine, Cambodia, 2013

Sharing an ice cream with one of my favourite tuk tuk drivers,
Cambodia, 2013

Lucy in the road with potholes, Ethiopia, 2016

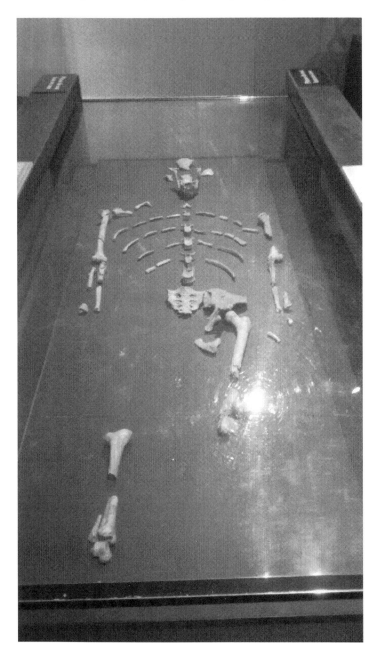

Visiting the Black Lion Hospital, Ethiopia, 2016

Teaching at the Black Lion Hospital, Ethiopia, 2016

Visiting the Yangon Children's Hospital, Myanmar, 2016

Discussing the difficulties in treating bone tumours, Myanmar, 2016

The railway journey of bone tumours, Myanmar, 2016

A collection of drawings, Myanmar, 2016

From where we came, a return to Haiti, 2017

The Rubik's Cube of trauma, Haiti, 2017

The surgical tourist, Haiti, 2017

Printed in Great Britain
by Amazon